theo

CHOCOLATE

CHOCOLATE

recipes & sweet secrets

FROM SEATTLE'S FAVORITE CHOCOLATE MAKER

Featuring 75 Recipes Both Sweet & Savory

DEBRA MUSIC AND JOE WHINNEY

with Leora Bloom
Photographs by Charity Burggraaf

SASQUATCH BOOKS
SEATTLE

Printed in China
Published by Sasquatch Books
19 18 17 16 15   9 8 7 6 5 4 3 2 1

Editor: Susan Roxborough
Production editor: Em Gale
Photography: Charity Burggraaf
Illustration and lettering: Emily Raffensperger
Design: Anna Goldstein
Food styling: Julie Hopper
Copyeditor: Diane Sepanski
Author photo courtesy of Theo Chocolate

Library of Congress Cataloging-in-Publication Data is available.
ISBN: 978-1-57061-997-7

Sasquatch Books
1904 Third Avenue, Suite 710
Seattle, WA 98101
(206) 467-4300
www.sasquatchbooks.com
custserv@sasquatchbooks.com

for henry,
our love for you has brought
out the best in us

♥ ♥ ♥

contents

♥ ♥ ♥

recipe list

♥ ♥ ♥

acknowledgments

♥ ♥ ♥

We humbly express our deepest gratitude to every Theo team member, for bringing their creativity and dedication daily, and ensuring we deliver products that reflect the highest quality standards while helping us create a culture that allows everyone to thrive. Our greatest reward is working alongside you every day.

To our farmers, suppliers, and partners, our trust and faith in you are well placed, and lay the very foundation for Theo's success.

We are grateful to the following chefs and companies for your beautiful contributions to this book, and proud to be associated with each and every one of you: Zoi Antonitsas, Clark and Tami Bowen, Jason Brzozowy, Casamigos Tequila, Chris Cosentino, Fran Costigan, Rome Doherty, Tom Douglas, Charlie Durham, Caffe Vita, Walter Edward, Maria Hines, Autumn Martin, Robin Martin, Naomi Pomeroy, Thierry Rautureau, Jennifer Shea, Adria Shimada, and Alex Williams.

Many thanks to Rebecca Pirwitz and Drew Zandonella-Stannard for packing countless bags of chocolate and organizing our exhaustive recipe testing.

A very special thank you to the members of our team and extended family who tested recipes for this book at home: Sarah Benner, Laura Botz, Nicole Cappozziello, Erin Connelly, Casey and Alexa Crane, Marc de Faye, Joanna Lepore Dwyer, Virginia Eader, Dave Follis, Chad Fuhreck, Tiffany Schmidt Gifford, Talya Gillman, Kelsey Hamilton, Christine Horne, Chuck Horne, Leslie Horne, Adria LaMorticella, Martha Lauer, Jessie Lundin, Dawn Macray, Dennis Macray, Nathan Palmer Royston, Katy Radtke, Bill Raes, Asha Sandhu, Tasha Stein, Cat Gipe Stewart, Max Stiles, Suzann Vaughn, Nate Watters, William West, and Christy Wicks.

A major shout-out to our confection team for all your help translating Theo recipes for home use, and for walking through the steps countless times to ensure we got them right: Laura Botz, Jesse Chappelle, Chad Fuhreck, Phil Gorbman, Steve Popplewell, Katy Radtke, and Suzann Vaughn.

Outside the factory, thanks to Megan Kirley, Chris Machielse, Marti McGinley, Allessandra McGinnis, Kristy Swanson, and Katie Wade for testing recipes. Your input was invaluable.

We'd also like to say thanks to Lauren Todes for her brilliant suggestions for the myriad ways to use dukkah, to Sarah Benner for sharing her macarons, to Sherry Segers for transcribing hours of interviews, and to Emily Raffensperger for her many artful contributions.

Theo is a family: a community of friends, contributors, and collaborators, all of whom make us what we are and inspire us to be better. Theo simply would not exist without the love and support of John and Mitzi Morris, Rich Falatico, Walt Maas, Scott Greenburg, Mike McConnell, Bob Burke, Peter Cheney, Suzie Burke, Michael Hebb, Dwight Richmond, Errol Schweizer, Ben Nauman, Gail Hudson, Dr. Jane Goodall, Whitney Williams, Harper McConnell, Heather Pfahl, Philip Betts, Ben Affleck, Zaara, Liz Pearl, Tera Beach, and all of Theo's investors.

Our undying gratitude and affection goes to Leora Bloom, for your culinary genius and perfectionism. We couldn't have, wouldn't have done it without you.

Charity Burggraaf, thank you for going above and beyond on multiple occasions to capture such delectability.

Deep thanks to the entire team at Sasquatch, led by the graciously wonderful Susan Roxborough, a skilled editor and an even better friend. Em Gale, thank you for your irrepressible spirit in the face of edits too numerous to count. Anna Goldstein, thank you for translating all our hard work into beautiful pages.

DM: Mom and Dad, your joie de vivre is unsurpassed.

Bradley Music, your love has made everything possible.

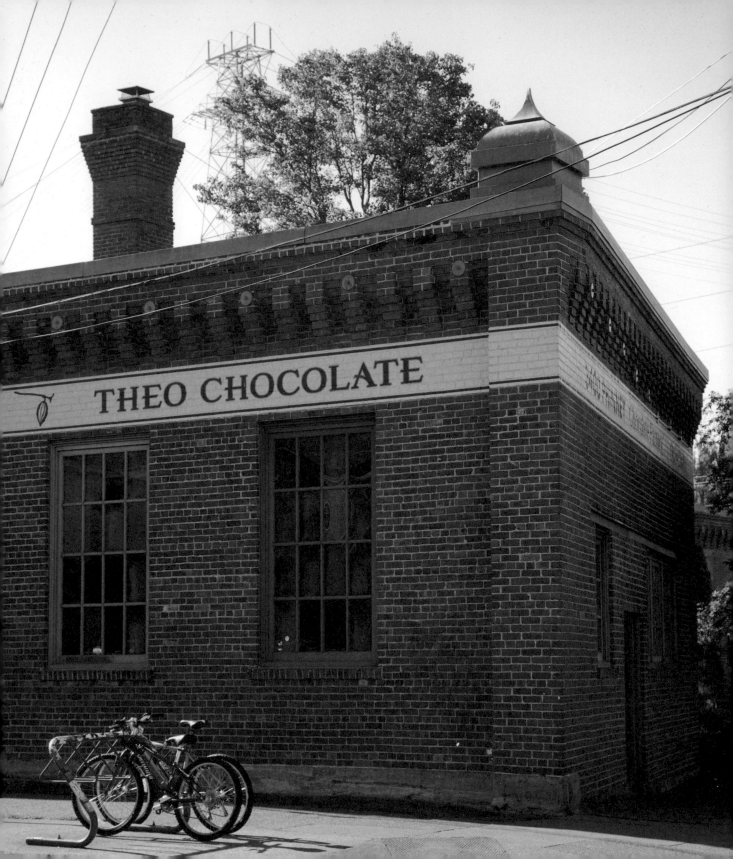

introduction: the theo story

♥ ♥ ♥

SHE SAID: DEBRA MUSIC

I grew up in Westchester, just north of New York City, the middle of three girls. My mom was (and still is) a talented cook, but she was always an equal-opportunity eater, and we were just as likely to have osso buco for dinner as to have a stash of Nacho Cheese Doritos in the cupboard. She taught us to enjoy our food, and she led by example. She's a healthy person, and I have countless memories of waiting idly in the summer heat while she did endless loops around the track at our local junior high school. But her love of exercise is only outpaced by the zeal with which she eats! Give the woman a steamed lobster, and when she's finished, all that's left is a dime-size pile of red shrapnel.

That's why when people ask me for my earliest chocolate memory (and they often do), my favorite one involves my mom. I remember looking for her one afternoon and finding her hiding out in my parents' bedroom, sitting cross-legged on the bed with a bag of mini Reese's Peanut Butter Cups open on her lap and wrappers strewn all over the floor. It made me smile then—and it still makes me smile today. Having been a working mom, I now understand her need for a few solitary moments; as a lifetime chocolate lover, I'm tickled to know that we share (along with our mutual love of exercise and great shoes) an appreciation for the sweetness and satisfaction chocolate can and does bring to so many of life's moments.

Flash-forward many years later, and unbeknownst to me, my life was about to be chocolate covered. When I first met Joe, I was in my late twenties, living and working in Cambridge, Massachusetts. Joe was living off the grid in Vermont, and he would leave during the cold months, headed for Belize, where he pursued all kinds of amazing adventures folded up in his passion for sustainable agriculture. I felt an immediate connection to Joe—the kind you can't explain with your rational mind—but as our lives were flowing in distinctly different directions at the time, we got to know each other as pen

Joe and Debra the year they were married.

pals, writing letters over the span of a year or so, without any agenda beyond the pleasure of exchanging ideas and musings.

Then one very rainy Saturday morning in the early spring of 1992, I opened the door to unexpectedly find Joe on my doorstep in a faded jean jacket (now co-opted by our nineteen-year-old son) and red Converse hightops. I was on my way to work, but he asked if he could crash with me for the night. I came home at the end of an exhausting, dreary day to a loft filled with the warm, earthy smells of freshly baked bread and roasted vegetables. I looked at Joe across a candlelit table, the earth moved, and that December we were married.

Long story short, though Joe and I love and appreciate each other to this day, we were not meant to be a married couple. Joe is fearless and loves adventure, works and plays hard, and is a huge risk taker. I'm a balance seeker, high on life, comfortable in the gray area, with both feet firmly planted on the ground. What we share—and have been able to preserve through all our relationship trials—is the mutual belief that, rooted in gratitude and armed with perseverance, resolve, and dedication, we can take the gifts we've been given in this life and use them to leave the world a slightly better place than we found it.

This shared idealism is what has enabled us to raise our son, Henry, together and preserve a sense of family for him as a divorced couple, and it's what enabled us to embark on the life-changing adventure we named Theo Chocolate. We often joke that Theo is our second child—and it's not so far from the truth. The psychic, emotional, physical, and financial commitment the company has required from both of us has been extraordinary—and the love, lessons, and satisfaction it has rewarded us with are equally astonishing.

Early in our married life Joe started his first company, the Organic Cacao Project. OCP's mission was to build a supply chain for bringing organic cocoa beans into the US market. When Joe started OCP, we were making our first home together in a cottage in Gloucester, Massachusetts, and when he wasn't typing up letters to US chocolate makers on his manual typewriter at our dining room table, he was working as a carpenter and a crewman on a lobster boat. I commuted into Cambridge every day for work, and for extra cash, on weekends I waitressed at the Old Firehouse, a tiny but popular restaurant in nearby Lanesville. I've always loved the pace and passion that comes with a working kitchen, as well as the immediacy of pleasing people through food—and the Old Firehouse was a hotbed for both. They were known far and wide for their French toast, and on weekends folks would line up around the block for it. The combined smells of that buttery griddle, salty sea air, and fresh strawberries are still with me today.

Henry was born in 1995, and Joe and I remained married for another year or so after that. Ultimately, our fundamental differences were too great for us to weather the demands of Joe's burgeoning business, his travel schedule, and the challenges we faced as new parents, and we divorced.

We established separate lives in the Boston area and figured out (through lots of trial and error) how to co-parent Henry, who is the light of both our lives. In early 2004, Joe came to me and told me about an opportunity he had to move to Seattle and start a chocolate factory. And not just any chocolate factory, but the kind he'd been dreaming about for more than a decade. He'd be able to build it from the ground up, to realize his vision of creating a stable supply chain that was fully transparent, where farmers were valued appropriately based on their input and the value-add that came with organic growing practices, proper environmental stewardship, and the resulting quality cocoa. As important was the fact that this new opportunity would allow him to build a consumer brand. Joe's experience with OCP had shown him that, when he was just supplying other manufacturers, he couldn't really move the needle. Profound change happens at the consumer level, and he wanted to communicate his message from the cocoa farm all the way through to the person buying the chocolate bar.

When he first approached me with this idea, I understood immediately that it involved me. Joe was not the kind of dad who would pick up and move across the country, away from his boy. So if Henry and I weren't moving to Seattle, he wasn't either.

At this point in my own career, I had a considerable background in both marketing and social marketing, which is basically taking marketing principles and applying them to public health issues. I loved the work I was doing, but it involved a great deal of travel—and home base for me could be anywhere. I was acutely aware of the fact that Joe had felt "stuck" in the Boston area since our divorce—and I couldn't bear the thought of keeping him stuck. Besides, I was ready for a change. The Boston winters had taken their toll on me, and adventure called. I told Joe I would consider the move, but I needed to visit Seattle first. I had been there only once before, when, on a lark, my friend Tonianne and I had decided to point randomly at a map and take a weekend trip wherever our fingers landed. It was fun, but my knowledge of the city was wildly limited.

Joe, Henry, and I arrived during a week in April, one of those weeks that get Seattleites through to summer. The sky was bright blue, the temperature balmy, the mountains clear and snowcapped, and everywhere I looked there was a profusion of spring flowers in full bloom. (I'm an avid gardener and a sucker for flowers.) I sat on a bench by Lake Union early one morning, a Seattle-caliber latte in hand, entranced as I watched a seaplane gently glide to a landing. I was utterly seduced by the sunlight playing off the water on the lake, accompanied by the gentle clang of halyards. I could live here, I thought to myself.

So I took a massive leap of faith. My friends and family thought I was nuts. After all, who moves across the country with their ex-husband? When we got to Seattle that summer, any doubts I had about uprooting Henry and myself evaporated quickly. I was grateful for the opportunity, and the open-endedness of everything reeked of possibility. My now husband of ten years, Brad, came into my life almost immediately upon arrival. Looking back, it feels a little like a good karma gift—Joe got to realize his dream, and I got happily-ever-after with a guy who was rock solid enough to fall in love with a woman who was starting a business with—not to mention living with—her ex-husband. (Joe and I felt it was best to live together for a while in order to help Henry, who was eight at the time, adjust to life in a new city without the added burden of two households.)

At first, Joe worked madly on building Theo, and I worked on the old house we'd moved into in Wallingford, which needed a lot of love. It was energizing to be in a new place with so much promise—and although it was also a little bit scary, I felt grateful to have had the courage to make such a dramatic change. Over time, and as things progressed at "The Chocolate Company"—our moniker in those early days—Joe asked me to join him at work. As Joe likes to tell it, he knew I "wouldn't let anything drop." The fact is, my background in social marketing and our shared ethos and work ethic, combined with the knowledge I had acquired vicariously about cocoa during our years together (not to mention my undying love for chocolate), made me a valuable collaborator for his new business venture. And Joe knew he could trust me.

I was really excited about building Theo. I've never been a person who can firewall my personal values from my professional life. It was thrilling on a philosophical level to be given the opportunity to create a brand that aspired to define the concept of "sustainable business" in a changing world. From day one, we made an unparalleled commitment to full transparency, accountability, compassion, and fun. There's a profound irony in the fact that, while chocolate is one of our most beloved indulgences, an expression of love in our culture, and a food that we use to comfort and celebrate ourselves, the conventional cocoa industry has been responsible for devastating environmental degradation and human exploitation for many decades.

Like so many of you reading this book, I've always been a chocolate devotee. I've eaten chocolate almost every day of my life. But the world is a much smaller place today than it once was, thanks to technology, and we have access to information at the tap of a keyboard. We know too much to continue to look away from the insidious impact of the conventional cocoa industry.

So I joined Joe at Theo. In order to realize our vision for full transparency, we knew we needed to educate consumers, so factory tours were always a cornerstone of our business plan. It would have been a lot less expensive and much easier for us to be in an industrial park rather than in the beautiful old historic building we occupy in Seattle's Fremont neighborhood, but in order to conduct tours, we needed to be in a walking district. The tours have been a huge hit since we launched them early in 2006—after all, the opportunity to go inside a working chocolate factory is a rare one. We've had hundreds of thousands of tour guests over the years, and we know it's a privilege to share our passion for what we do with people on a daily basis. Ultimately the aim of our tours is to unlock the mystery of chocolate making for consumers, and to help our visitors understand that their consumer choices have an impact on other human beings and the planet we all share.

During the first couple of years, I did many of the jobs there were to do, from scraping cocoa butter off the factory floor to gingerly placing endless trays of confections into little paper cups. I vividly remember waking suddenly from sleep one night (à la Miss Clavel in the *Madeleine* books I loved as a girl) with the instant awareness that I had failed to turn the warming tank for our enrober back on before leaving for the day. This would result in a mass of solid chocolate and a burned-out motor in the morning. I jumped in my car in my pajamas and drove to the factory at 3 a.m. to turn it on.

When we were first conceiving our brand, we sequestered ourselves on a friend's houseboat on Lake Union with easel pads and Magic Markers. I still have the yellow loose-leaf paper on which Joe and I sketched our ideas for the Theo logo with a pencil, and the subsequent design boards our amazing designer, Zaara (KittenChops.com), presented to us after we hired her to bring our ideas to life.

Although the factory was supposed to be up and running within a year, it actually took two. I'll never forget walking our very first batch of chocolate up to the PCC market in Fremont, where they took it from our hands and put it directly on their shelf. That was an amazing day. But it was just one of so many amazing days to come.

In the end, I'm most humbled by the fact that we create delicious, award-winning products that make people happy. Together with our team we've had so many surprise-and-delight moments in and out of the factory over the years, with products like Ghost Chili caramels, Big Daddy Marshmallows, and Fig, Fennel & Almond bars. We make the best brownies in the world. Our drinking chocolate is life changing. So this cookbook is a long overdue opportunity for us to share with you all the creativity, passion, and love our team has conjured in our kitchen over the years. The recipes very intentionally run the gamut from simple to sophisticated, so you can challenge yourself or just whip up something yummy when the mood strikes. Either way, we're grateful to you for helping us write the next chapter of the Theo story.

♥ ♥ ♥

HE SAID: JOE WHINNEY

I never imagined while growing up in northeast Philadelphia that anything as simple as chocolate would turn out to be such an adventure. As a kid, chocolate was something that I stole from my brother on Halloween. It was brown and cheap and sweet. There was nothing that connected my chocolate candy to rain forests or indigenous tribes or endangered animals. The idea that chocolate has corrupted governments and fostered slavery seems surreal when I remember myself as that kid in Philly who loved those sweet chocolaty treats.

I knew from a young age that I was a little different. I knew that I wasn't cut out to have a job that was only about making money. Money has never been a motivator for me. I wanted to follow my passions and have adventures. I wanted to see the world, but not as a tourist. When I traveled, I wanted to become a part of a place as much as possible. I was committed to trying to experience the world from the perspective of the people I was visiting. To this day, if I'm going to be in the world, I want to *be in* the world, not as a spectator but as a full-fledged participant.

I was fortunate that from the start my family instilled in me the belief that I could do anything I set my mind to. They also taught me that it was important to do the right thing, always, no matter the cost. Because of my family, I grew up believing that anything I could imagine was possible and that living with integrity was more valuable than any amount of fame or fortune. I wish I could say that I've lived up to these beliefs. Over the years, and through many endeavors, I've failed in ways both large and small. I've bargained; I've traded; I have straight-up prayed for forgiveness. But through all of my trials I have always had an unwavering north star, a way point: a strong belief that I will make it better than it was. I still believe this.

As a teenager I didn't feel the need to be grounded by the mortal demands of high school (often to the dismay and frustration of my dear mother). I wanted to travel, have fun with my friends, and explore all that the world had to offer. As the senior class president in high school I thought that it was a great idea to drop out just before graduation and start my adventures.

I made my way to New England via an old VW bug with no brakes. After working as a carpenter and a back man on a lobster boat, I decided it was time to have a real adventure. I was in my early twenties, and inspired by my love of open water and boats, I decided to sail around Belize and parts of Guatemala. I wanted to experience a part of the world that was, at that time, still wild and beautiful.

The more time I spent in southern Belize, where the rain forests of the Maya Mountains meet the ocean and the world's second largest barrier reef, the more I wanted to do something that might contribute to the preservation and culture of this amazing place. I volunteered for a small conservation foundation, the Tropical Conservation Foundation (TNC), and found myself a remarkable mentor, botanist, and visionary, Mark Cohen. I had a strong back and was up for anything. There I had a deep immersion in permaculture and in traditional Mayan ways of life, from hunting and farming to building dug-out canoes carved from giant trees.

Learning to harvest cocoa was amazing. I had no idea where cocoa came from, how it was grown, what the lives were like of the people who grew cocoa—it was all new. There I was in this tropical forest with Dr. Seuss–like trees towering overhead and wild birds calling all around. The sunlight scattered over moss, giant composting leaves, and countless creatures that were living off of and digesting the forest floor.

Cocoa fruit, or pods, grows right off the sides of trees as oval gourds. The farmers would use poles with blades on the ends to slice the pods off the trees. As the pods tumbled down I would run around trying to gather them up as fast as they fell. I would pile the pods up until all of the nearby trees were harvested. I sat with the farmers to crack open the pods and scoop out the pulp-covered seeds with my hands until my rice sack backpack was full. As we scooped, we sucked on the seeds, enjoying the sweet fruit.

Leaning up against a massive tree buttress, listening to the sounds of the forest, savoring the sweetness of the fruit, I fell in love. This was chocolate. It is through chocolate that I was taught and experienced firsthand the ways in which all of life is interconnected—an understanding that has stayed with me and informed almost all of my life choices since that time. I was deeply inspired by everything from the New England songbirds that winter in tropical Central American cocoa forests to the wild tiny stingless bees that the Maya revered as sacred and which made honey that some believed produced mystical experiences when ingested. I discovered the interdependence of the amazing lives we live, with every other living organism.

I didn't know then that my first day working on a cocoa farm on the edge of the rain forest was the first day of what is now twenty-three-plus years in the chocolate industry. I didn't know then that those early days would profoundly shape the rest of my life. Back then I could not begin to imagine a day, many harrowing years later, when yummy chocolate recipes would be shared between loved ones, friends, cooks, and chocolate devotees because, in part, I decided to have a little adventure.

Ultimately, I saw firsthand the horrible impact that the chocolate industry has had on cocoa growers and the landscape that they steward. After spending a lot of time in Central America and learning more and more about the social and environmental consequences of the conventional cocoa industry, I decided that I needed to do something. In 1994 I brought the very first container of organic cocoa into North America from Costa Rica, with the help of Roberto Mack and Walter Rodriguez, true cocoa pioneers. Perhaps naively, I believed that if I could help connect consumers who wanted environmentally sustainable food, grown by farmers who were paid enough for their crops that they could have a good quality of life and hope for the future, that I would be able to show the big chocolate companies that chocolate making could help make the world a better place. How hard could that be?

I built a business that was paying farmers premiums for their crops while supplying chocolate and cocoa products to the leading organic food brands in North America. We had a lot of growth and I invested a lot of time just building the supply chain of high-quality organic cocoa. My cocoa pursuits led me to West Africa, where most of the world's cocoa is produced. I thought that I had seen poverty and desperation in parts of Latin America. It was nothing compared to what I experienced in Africa. My first of many trips to Africa in the midnineties was to Ghana, the second largest producer of cocoa in the world. I had never seen such extreme poverty. The consequences of the cocoa industry were shocking. On that first visit I promised myself I would do everything I possibly could to change the way the conventional cocoa industry does business.

It seemed clear to me that the only way to accomplish this was to lead by example and build a successful business that made and sold a great product from raw materials at a fair price, leaving everyone in the supply chain all the way through to the end consumer better off. I had to build a company that would communicate directly with consumers through a brand and product that people could believe in.

Theo would not exist if I hadn't met Debra. Debra was sharing a house with a friend of mine in Cambridge, Massachusetts, when I stopped in for a warm meal and bed on my way to Central America from Vermont. I could not have imagined, that night on Green Street when we first met in Cambridge, how important Debra would become to me.

We kept in touch via correspondence and a spring or two later, driving back to Vermont, I made sure to visit her. She had moved into a loft in what used to be called the combat zone in Boston. The loft was sprawling and perfectly shabby chic, complete with a swing and giant windows looking out on industrial south Boston. I didn't know it yet but I was falling in love with the lovely young women in thrift store dresses and Doc Martens.

I was living off the grid in Vermont on seventy-two acres at the very end of the road, in an old three-story ice house resurrected and rebuilt in the middle of an heirloom apple orchard with views of the Chelsea valley. I didn't have a telephone and the only way to reach me was by mail or getting word to a friend down the road or in town. It was spring and morel season. Debra came to visit and we went mushroom foraging for breakfast one morning. When I saw Debra marching through the forest holding the hem of her dress to make a billowing basket full of morels, I knew I was in love.

We split our romance between her loft and my paradise, aptly named Prospero's Island. We did the only thing any reasonable and rational people would do; we got married eight months after our first kiss.

Henry, our son, was born in 1995 and we separated in 1996. I was building a business, traveling the world to work with farmers in West Africa and Latin America, and suddenly figuring out how to be a single father. Debra was always supportive of me as a father, and I knew that I could trust her completely and in any circumstance.

I began to dream about building Theo in the late nineties. It took several years before I would find the right investors and community of people who could believe in my vision. It takes a very special group to build a business that's designed to be successful long-term and that values the success of its social and environmental mission as much as its financial profit. Seattle offered that in the form of investors, a beautiful building, and a long growing season that would allow us to source organic ingredients, locally.

When I first told Debra that I wanted to move to Seattle to build a chocolate factory but would not go unless Henry would come with me, which meant that she would have to come too, Debra didn't laugh me out of her living room. I can't say that I was surprised that

Debra would consider moving across the country with her ex-husband and eight-year-old kid. She has always been a brave and strong woman.

We moved to Seattle in August of 2004. Debra was a marketing consultant and was able to continue her work remotely. I set out to build Theo. Job one was to convert an old trolley barn and former brewery into a chocolate factory. I spent my days and nights planning construction, sourcing equipment, reconnecting with old cocoa friends to source raw materials, and figuring out the money needed to do all of the above. As soon as it was time to figure out how we would market and sell our chocolate, assuming we would actually be able to make it, I needed someone who I could trust implicitly and someone who had the experience, smarts, and tenacity that this start-up would require. I turned to Debra. At this point in my life there was no one else who had been through so much with me.

Debra has seen me at my absolute very best and my very worst. I knew that if I wanted Theo to be a success I needed her on board. By the time the first bars rolled off the belt in February of 2006, Debra had worked on the chocolate bar molding line, commandeered our confection enrober, was our entire shipping department, and played den mother to the crazy band of characters that we had become starting up the business.

This group of very brave people—who invested their hard-earned money and worked long hours to bring Theo to life—shared my vision that chocolate could help change the world. As a small group of believers we suspended common sense and warnings from friends and family and built the world's first organic and Fair Trade–certified chocolate factory.

Today, we sell our product in a multitude of retail and grocery stores, our team is nearing one hundred people in Seattle, and we are impacting thousands of cocoa-farming families in Africa and Latin America. We still have so much work to do, but I feel incredibly fortunate that I have the opportunity to work with amazing people like Debra and so many others. If success is measured by the company you keep, then Theo and I have been successful beyond anything I could ever have imagined.

I'm exceedingly proud of this cookbook. Not because I wrote it—I didn't. But because in some small way I've done something that helps amazing people do amazing things, like create this book. This adventure of mine might help do something good in the world after all. I invite you to join me for a little while. All you have to do is go make some chocolate cake!

our mission

♥ ♥ ♥

We are Theo Chocolate.

We're passionate about chocolate.
And changing the world.

We're committed to creating amazing flavors.
And a lasting legacy.

We're here to make people happy.
And make a difference.
We hope you'll join us.

making bean-to-bar chocolate

♥ ♥ ♥

Each bite of Theo chocolate connects you with our process and our story—from the farmers who grew the beans to the people who roast, mill, conch, and temper them in our factory. You can taste the rich and complex blend of cocoa beans that gives our chocolate its character, the care and precision that go into making each bar, and the creativity and joy that lead to our unique flavor profiles. Each bite of Theo chocolate is an experience— and your experience is proof of our commitment to creating the best chocolate in the world.

♥ ♥ ♥

FROM BEAN . . .

Harvest and Fermentation

The chocolate tree is a small, shade-loving tree whose fruit sprouts directly from its trunk and branches, and ripens into pods the size and shape of footballs, with deep, smooth ridges from end to end. As they ripen, they turn shades of yellow, orange, and red.

Cocoa pods are harvested by hand, cut from the trees with a machete and cracked open to expose the sticky white fruit inside, called mucilage, that covers the seeds. The mucilage is scooped out and piled into large boxes with holes in the bottom to allow for drainage. Wild yeasts feed on the sugars in the mucilage, creating alcohols that turn into acids, which are then fed on by bacteria that ferment the beans. During this process the beans are frequently turned to oxygenate the pile and ensure that all the beans in the box are evenly fermented. Proper fermentation is a critical first step in the flavor development of quality cocoa beans.

Cocoa pods growing on a cocoa tree.

Colorful ripened pods.

During the fermentation process, the cocoa bean pile becomes hot and smells pungent and sour. Proper fermentation takes about a week, at which point the mucilage will have liquefied and mostly drained away. Once fermentation is complete, the beans cool down and the pungent smell dissipates, although a vinegary trace scent often remains.

who is theo?

The name Theo comes from *Theobroma Cacao*, the Latin genus and species of the cocoa tree. We named the company after the tree because it's at the very heart of all we do! Don't miss the design detail in our logo: the "o" is shaped like a cocoa pod.

Drying and Sorting

Post fermentation, the beans need to be dried to prevent rotting and mold. Typically they are laid out on drying tables, ideally on elevated screens so that air can circulate around them. They are left to dry completely, with an occasional stirring, for about a week. The drying and stirring process also serves to remove foreign materials like rocks or sticks that naturally occur in the drying environment. Often it's at this point that the cooperative or exporter will inspect the beans, cutting samples in half to check fermentation levels and look for defects. Ultimately the beans are sorted based on quality.

Transporting the Beans

Once the dried beans have been sorted, they are scooped into the burlap (or other) sacks that are so commonly associated with coffee and cocoa. The bags are transported, often via very complicated routes on circuitous and rough roads, to the port from which they will depart. There, they are loaded into shipping containers to begin their very long journey to our factory. Although it takes about three weeks for beans to get, say, from a farm in Peru to Seattle, the journey is more complicated for our Congolese beans and can take three months or more.

a note on cacao vs. cocoa

Most commonly, these terms are interchangeable. Here at Theo we fondly refer to the source of all chocolate, the fruit of *Theobroma cacao*, as "cacao" while it is on the tree and while it is undergoing fermentation and drying, but once it arrives at our factory we call it "cocoa." However, for the purposes of this book, we have simplified matters and just call it "cocoa" at every stage.

what is organic?

We subscribe to the most stringent definition of organic. We only use non-GMO foods, grown without synthetic pesticides or chemical fertilizers, that have not been irradiated or exposed to industrial solvents or food additives. Every Theo ingredient has been verified as organic (except for items where this is not possible, such as salt, or where such verification is very elusive, such as honey), and we work with farmers and suppliers to ensure these standards are maintained.

Our work with our farmer partners supports their ability to utilize sustainable growing practices that benefit both our fragile environmental ecosystem and the people inhabiting our planet. We focus on integrated pest management, which protects farmers and the environment from damaging pesticides; biodiverse farming, which provides habitat for many species such as migratory birds; and reforestation, which helps offset worldwide air pollution and has a positive impact on global warming.

♥ ♥ ♥

what is fair trade?

Fair Trade is an international system with certifications that guarantee producers have been paid a price that enables positive economic growth for the individual and the region. The social benefits of Fair Trade are far-reaching. Farmers benefiting from the Fair Trade system are better able to provide their families with adequate nutrition, access to health care, and education, ultimately opening up a world of opportunities. Fair Trade enables farmers to take their livelihoods to the next level of sophistication, blending modern farming techniques with artisanal practices, while participating in greater social change through the Fair Trade organization.

♥ ♥ ♥

what is non-gmo?

Non-GMO means that a food is free from genetically modified organisms. Genetically modified organisms are experimental plants or animals that have been engineered in a laboratory with DNA from other plants, animals, bacteria, or viruses. GMOs have not been proven safe, and their long-term consequences on our health and environment have not been adequately investigated. Currently, most US states and Canadian provinces don't require labeling of genetically engineered foods. In forty other countries, including Australia, Japan, and all European Union nations, there are significant restrictions or outright bans on the production of GMOs because they're not considered proven safe. At Theo we believe consumers have the right to know what's in their food, and we've made a commitment to non-GMO verification of our products.

a short history of chocolate

Archaeological evidence suggests that humans have been consuming the fruit of *Theobroma cacao* since as early as 1900 BC, although it was probably the sweet pulp that surrounds the beans that was first eaten or fermented, rather than the beans themselves.

According to anthropologists and food historians Sophie Coe and Michael Coe, authors of the incredibly comprehensive volume *The True History of Chocolate*, it was the Olmec people of Mesoamerica, the first civilization in the Americas, who first domesticated *Theobroma cacao*. They passed the tradition to the Maya, who used cocoa as trading currency and enjoyed it as a frothy, spicy drink. It played an important part in their religious ceremonies and was prized by their kings.

In turn, the Maya introduced cocoa to the Aztec, who collected their taxes and tributes from people who lived in cocoa-growing regions in the form of cocoa beans. The Aztec put such a high value on cocoa beans that they ceased to be a food for the masses and were reserved for royalty and nobility. As the Coes point out, when an Aztec drank chocolate, it was like someone today using a twenty-dollar bill to light his cigar!

When the Spanish defeated the Aztec in 1521, they brought cocoa and other goods back to Spain. The Spanish heated it, someone added sugar, and its popularity exploded across Europe.

These days we consume a great deal more chocolate in solid form than liquid, but although we've streamlined chocolate production to such an extent that there are few places in the world where you can't find it, *Theobroma cacao* still only grows 20 degrees north and south of the equator.

. . . TO BAR

Once the beans arrive in Seattle, our work to transform them begins. Our factory is a working testament to our belief in the marriage between artisanal methods and innovation. It occupies a historic brick building in the Fremont neighborhood, originally built in 1905 to house streetcars, called the Fremont Barn. The occupant before us was the Redhook Brewery, who vacated in 2002. In the early years, passersby would often tap on our windows looking for beer—but they quickly overcame any disappointment when we offered them chocolate instead.

Almost every piece of the original equipment we used to make chocolate was sourced as surplus or secondhand. Our first acquisitions came from Germany and Norway, primarily from old factories that were either closing or modernizing. Some machines arrived in working order, while others were delivered requiring updates, refurbishment, or modification to suit the needs of our particular bean-to-bar process. As Europe uses different voltages than the United States, even the best machines had to be rewired to operate here. All told, it took about a year to source and install our chocolate-making equipment. We continue to add more machines as our production has increased, but all of those first quirky machines are still going strong.

How We Make Chocolate at Theo

The many details that make up chocolate manufacturing include quality of incoming raw materials; formulations we develop that ensure our chocolate is decidedly, uniquely delicious; and process engineering that underpins our ability to consistently manufacture our finished product to an ideal particle size, moisture and fat content, and—ultimately—flavor.

STEP 1: CHECK FOR DEFECTS

As soon as the beans arrive in Fremont from our warehouse, we offload them and one of our operators pulls samples to perform a "cut test" (by actually cutting a sampling of beans in half and looking at them) to assess quality. This includes determining the percentages of the varying degrees of fermentation of the cocoa beans as well as checking for flaws such as mold or other factors that will impart undesirable flavor attributes to our finished chocolate.

STEP 2: CLEAN AND DE-STONE

Once the beans pass our quality standards, they are cleaned and de-stoned. After all, the beans are grown in humid tropical ecosystems, and they are collected, fermented, and dried at the farm or community level. The cleaning and de-stoning is a dry process in which foreign matter is removed as the beans are conveyed through machines with vibrating screen decks and chambers under vacuum. Every cocoa bean goes through this process.

STEP 3: ROAST

We currently have two direct-fire ball roasters that utilize a convection process. The heat produced by the burners in these roasters goes directly into the rotating ball-shaped chamber that holds the beans. We use these types of roasters because they are configured to allow for a lot of flexibility in operator input, meaning we can develop the greatest potential flavor from the beans. Both of our roasters are real workhorses, unique in appearance, and still going strong after more than fifty years.

Roasting beans in our Barth Sirocco ball roaster.

Cocoa beans cooling off after roasting in the cooling tray.

The primary objective of roasting is to develop flavor in the beans, coaxing out chocolaty components while preserving each bean's unique characteristics. At Theo, we roast the whole cocoa bean. Our roasting experts need to consider bean fermentation levels as well as the desired flavor elements for each particular batch of finished chocolate. They draw on years of experience to develop the flavor nuances of beans from different cocoa-growing regions of the world. Unlike coffee, cocoa beans are roasted low and slow, at temperatures no higher than approximately 320 degrees F, for anywhere between thirty-five and sixty-five minutes. The roast time and temperature varies depending on bean origin, properties, and our desired flavor profile.

Besides flavor development, there are two additional goals our roasters must achieve. The first is to reduce the moisture content of the beans from 6 or 7 percent (upon arrival at Theo) to 1 percent. The second goal is to reduce the microbiological activity in the beans. Cocoa beans are a fermented product, they are frequently harvested by hand, and they travel thousands of miles over the course of many weeks from a humid environment. Heating them over an extended period of time reduces bacteria, ensuring they are safe for consumption. All three roasting goals are equally important to ensure that we have good material with which to make outstanding products.

STEP 4: WINNOW

The beans come out of the roaster piping hot and are released directly into a cooling tray. Once they're cool, we transfer them via a conveying system into the winnower, also known as a "cracker and fanner." The winnower breaks the whole beans into small pieces called nibs and allows for the removal of the papery husk. Nibs are great for eating out of hand or cooking with (you'll discover them featured in a lot of recipes in this book). A portion of our nibs are packaged for sale, but the bulk of them move on to be milled for chocolate making.

STEP 5: MILL

Cocoa nibs are milled in two stages. The first stage takes place in a stone mill, which contains two giant stones: one fixed and another that's attached to a motor shaft that spins around. The nibs are pulled down into the gap between the stones, where they are ground up. The grinding process reduces the particle size of the cocoa solids and, in conjunction with the heat generated, frees up the cocoa butter contained in the beans. The result is a liquid we call cocoa liquor (although there's no alcohol in it; it's just industry terminology).

The cocoa liquor is then pumped into a second mill, called a ball mill, where the cocoa solids, suspended in the cocoa butter, are interspersed with thousands of tiny steel balls that are being agitated. This process serves to reduce the particle size of the cocoa solids to about that of plant pollen.

The benefits of milling to an extremely fine specification are primarily sensory—the finer you mill a particle, the greater dispersion you'll have on your palate when you eat it. For example, compare the experience of eating a spoonful of coarsely ground versus smooth peanut butter: the finer the particle size, the smoother the mouthfeel, and the more intense the flavor. Our goal is to achieve the maximum presence of cocoa flavor and a smooth, sensual chocolate experience.

STEP 6: MIX AND REFINE

Once we've milled the cocoa solids into cocoa liquor, we add coarse granulated sugar to a portion of it, utilizing the fat content in the liquor to carry the sugar through rolling refiners. These are long rollers that turn and grind against each other at high speed in opposing directions to mechanically break down the sugar particles. This process also occurs in two stages, with our three- and five-roll refiners. It's fascinating to watch the mix of liquor and sugar start as a wet paste, then transform into a fine, dry powder we call cocoa flake. This change occurs as the sugar is broken down into smaller and smaller particles; more and more surface area is created and ultimately the refined sugar particles completely absorb the chocolate liquor.

Cocoa nibs coming off the winnower.

Refined cocoa flake.

From the finish refiner, the cocoa flake goes up a conveyor belt into the conch, where it's heated and then slowly combined with more chocolate liquor—as much as is required to make each particular batch of chocolate. For example, more liquor will be introduced if we're making 85 percent chocolate than if we're making 70 percent chocolate.

The conching process both homogenizes the material and provides our final opportunity to develop flavor according to our high standards for flavor complexity.

We slowly add cocoa liquor, and the chocolate flake goes from what we call the dry phase to the plastic phase—the mass at this point has the consistency of clay. There are giant paddles inside the conch that work the claylike mass against the sidewalls to ensure that all the solids, especially the sugar, are evenly coated in fat. The third phase of conching is the liquid phase. We add a massive amount of mechanical and thermal energies, which means we get the mass really, really hot and agitate it with giant stirrers. This action evenly coats all the solid particles with fat, resulting in a smooth mouthfeel.

Depending on the origin, batch size, cocoa percentage, and recipe, we'll conch for anywhere from twelve to forty-eight hours, in the most extreme cases.

Cocoa flake making its way to the conch.

Finished chocolate.

During this process, we strictly control temperature and airflow. We introduce and remove air in order to remove unwanted volatiles from the cocoa mass. Volatiles are organic compounds with very low boiling points—most aromas are volatiles. There are over 600 chemical compounds in chocolate, and not all of them taste or smell good. By subjecting them to a certain amount of heat, agitation, and airflow, we remove the ones we don't want. For example, cocoa beans are a fermented product, and one of the largest by-products of fermentation is acetic acid (the main component of vinegar); safe to say, we don't want that in our chocolate. When you take a Theo factory tour, you'll no doubt experience a symphony of aromas.

The conching process is long and requires a delicate balance. Overconching can result in a fairly neutral and flat-tasting finished product. There's a bit of magic combined with chemistry in the marriage between roasting and conching that results in chocolate with depth, complexity, and an array of desirable flavors.

Once the conching is complete, we add organic vanilla bean for flavor and more cocoa butter to reduce the viscosity of the liquid chocolate so that it will flow into our bar molds and spread out as well as to enhance mouthfeel. Many chocolate manufacturers add soy lecithin to adjust viscosity, but being the purists we are, we stick to organic cocoa butter (see Chocolate Types and Percentages, page 23, for more information on soy lecithin and what we put in our chocolate).

STEP 8: TEMPER

Each batch of chocolate flows through pipelines into a holding tank, where it's kept warm and agitated to prevent the solids from separating until we're ready to temper it and mold it into bars. If you get a chance to visit our factory, remember to look up at the hundreds and hundreds of feet of pipeline running overhead—there's one full pound of chocolate in every ten inches!

The tempering process is what gives chocolate its shine and snap and makes the finished product shelf stable. The proper temper means the chocolate will melt at a higher temperature. It involves heating the chocolate until it's hot enough that the crystalline structure formed by the cocoa-fat molecules breaks up, and then cooling it aggressively to a very precise temperature, causing the fat's crystalline structure to realign and lock together. Our tempering machine can continuously process almost two thousand pounds of chocolate per hour.

STEP 9: ADD INCLUSIONS AND MOLD INTO BARS

Once the chocolate is in temper, we warm it just enough to maintain its liquid state. This gives us enough time to deposit it into bar molds and pass them on a track over vibrators that settle the chocolate and remove any air bubbles. If we're molding flavored bars, we add any additional ingredients (everything from dried fruits and nuts to sea salt or curry powder) just before the chocolate gets deposited into the molds.

STEP 10: COOL AND PACKAGE

The filled chocolate bar molds travel along a conveyor belt through a cooling tunnel. The solid bars are flipped out and checked for quality. Once they pass the test, they're wrapped, boxed, and ready to be shared and enjoyed.

THEO SOURCING PRACTICES

The work of cocoa farmers lays the foundation for, motivates, and inspires everything we do at Theo. We're committed to full transparency in our relationships, and are always open to new and interesting sources of cocoa, as well as new partners who share our commitment to quality, environmental sustainability, and ethical business practices, with whom we can develop long-standing relationships. We actively engage with our farmer partners throughout the world to help ensure our mutual success. We provide a secure market through cocoa contracts that span each harvest with pricing based on quality—the higher the quality of cocoa, the higher the premium payment to farmers. We support each farmer group with the tools and/or technical assistance they may need to produce the highest quality cocoa possible, based on their unique circumstances. Our goal is always to help our farmer partners achieve the highest value for their crop.

Evaluating Cocoa Beans

Ultimately, chocolate quality is determined by the marriage between the cocoa genetics, the quality of the farmer's post-harvest handling, and the roasting and conching processes at our factory. After we determine that a particular region has promising genetics, we then evaluate the quality of the post-harvest process (which includes fermentation and drying) at the farm or community level. We look for the percentage of properly fermented cocoa, any defects such as mold or insect damage, and bean size. In the end, flavor is what is most important to us and measuring certain physical characteristics can give us and the producers clear empirical information to work with in order to understand flavor potential.

Proper fermentation is an extremely important part of processing cocoa and can be evaluated through a cocoa quality analysis or "cut test" once the beans have been dried. Cocoa beans fresh from the pod, when cut in half, are bright purple, solid, and soft. By contrast, properly fermented and dried beans will have a consistent chocolate-brown color, ranging from light to dark, with well-defined cracks and fissures, like little canyons and natural break points (blond cocoa beans can be well fermented without a brown color). Well-fermented beans may have a deep cocoa or nutty aroma, while poorly fermented beans may have a much more pungent vinegary smell because their acid levels are too high. We provide training to co-op, export, and community leaders on how to conduct their own cut tests. These trainings empower farmers to assess the value of their own crops.

At the factory, we consistently receive bean samples from cocoa-growing regions worldwide, and we regularly make lab samples of chocolate liquor in order to provide feedback on flavor and quality to their growers. Regardless of whether or not we are in a position to buy the cocoa, we provide feedback because of our commitment to providing support for farmers and our desire for full transparency in our supply chain. If we believe there's a potential for high-quality cocoa and for Theo to have a positive impact on the communities involved, we'll explore the path forward relative to both quality and logistics.

Sharing the Taste of Chocolate

Just as most chocolate consumers don't know where cocoa comes from—or the environmental, economic, and geographical challenges of the farmers who grow it—neither do most cocoa farmers have exposure to the average chocolate consumer. In many of the cocoa-growing regions of the world, cocoa farmers have little understanding of what happens to their cocoa beans after they've sold them and, in fact, have never tasted well-tempered and high-quality finished chocolate—some have never tasted chocolate at all!

One of the most important (and moving) aspects of our farmer education program is sharing that taste. Eating is an intimate experience, and by bringing farmers closer to the finished product—literally the fruits of their labor—we help connect them with chocolate consumers at the other end of the value chain. This mirrors the education we provide chocolate consumers through our factory tours. We hope to create a deeper sense of purpose for farmers and a more meaningful experience of chocolate for everyone.

The Theo model is designed to illuminate and adequately reflect the true value of farmer contributions, to elevate them in the supply chain, and to equip farmers to invest in their cocoa as a stable source of livelihood.

Fostering Healthy Trees

Cocoa, by biological design, is an understory crop in the rain forest and thrives in biodiverse forests. Quality cocoa comes from a combination of good genetics, climate, geography, and farmer practices that result in healthy trees. We collaborate with and support organizations that teach farmers Good Agricultural Practices (GAP). These include proper pruning and encouraging farmers to establish vertical biodiversity, which cocoa trees need both to provide shade and to form a layer of fallen branches and leaves that suffocate weeds. This layer then decays into a warm, nutrient-rich mulch that holds water, feeds the trees, and provides a home for the tiny midge flies that pollinate them.

Promoting Organic Cocoa Beans

Currently, the organic cocoa market represents a very small share of the total cocoa market. At Theo we buy only traceable, certified-organic, Fair Trade beans. Most of the world's cocoa comes from West Africa, where many development programs are geared toward farmers increasing chemical inputs to control pests and diseases on the trees and to increase yields.

Theo's quality-driven pricing program, with technical assistance for farmers, cooperatives, and exporters, empowers every stakeholder in our cocoa supply chain to test for quality, properly take cocoa bean samples, and improve post-harvest practices to meet our standards. All of this is designed to close the information gap between origin and our factory, and help farmers cultivate the finest cocoa possible.

how you can help

Our global travels have taught us that everyone has the same hopes and dreams. We all want our families to be healthy. We want to have a sense of purpose in life. We want to believe that if we work hard, our futures are bright. And we want to feel a sense of connection to the world around us. The closer we are to the people who grow our food the more connected we feel. The more connected we feel, the more likely we are to enjoy the lives we are given. Chocolate may play a relatively small part in our lives, but if in partaking in this lovely tiny indulgence we can make a real difference in someone else's life, it can become much more than a momentary pleasure.

Most cocoa farmers, whether part of a cooperative system or not, are economically disadvantaged, and although Theo works to partner with farmers in a meaningful way and pays premiums based on quality far above and beyond the Fair Trade premium standards, ours is a unique business model in the multi-billion-dollar global chocolate industry. We are working hard every day to transform the cocoa industry from the inside out—but true change will only occur when consumers demand it. For cocoa farmers to be successful, consumers need to insist on high-quality, ethical chocolate with verified transparency that ensures farmers are benefiting from premium prices.

This is why consumer education is a cornerstone of our business. We welcome visitors from all over the world to our factory every single day, sharing our knowledge of the chocolate industry and the magic of how cocoa beans are transformed into chocolate. Our guests return home knowing a little bit more about what high-quality chocolate tastes like; why standards like organic, Fair Trade, and non-GMO matter (for more information on these standards, see the definitions of organic, Fair Trade, and non-GMO on page 4); and how to create positive change in the world by choosing products aligned with their values, essentially voting with their dollars. We hope to see you at Theo some day soon!

the basics of working with chocolate

♥ ♥ ♥

You don't need to be a scientist or a pastry chef to work with chocolate, but a little information and a small dose of patience will go a long way to ensuring your success in the kitchen. So although we know that the siren call of the recipes beckons enticingly, we suggest you grab a bar of your favorite Theo chocolate, put your feet up, and settle in for a quick lesson on how to work with chocolate. Your patience will be rewarded ten-fold.

♥ ♥ ♥

HOW TO TASTE CHOCOLATE

At Theo we taste and approve each batch of chocolate before it's molded for further use in our specialty, culinary, or chocolate bar products. Although we have formulations, cocoa beans are an agricultural product, so there is always some variation in the finished chocolate. Making chocolate is a craft in much the same way as making wine—someone's palate is always involved. We let the cocoa beans guide our recipes: some chocolate lends itself to standing alone, and others pair well with inclusions such as nuts, fruits, or spices. Some of our formulations blend beans with complementary attributes, and some highlight the attributes of beans from a single origin.

LOOK: Dark chocolate should have a rich brown color (color will vary with bean origin and cocoa percentage) and a beautifully glossy surface.

BREAK: A clean, crisp snap reveals that the chocolate is in temper, meaning the cocoa butter, or natural fat of the cocoa bean, has bonded with the cocoa solids. A proper temper gives chocolate its optimal texture.

TASTE: Let a small piece of chocolate melt in your mouth. Is it creamy and smooth, or slightly dry and complex? If the chocolate has inclusions, how do they affect texture or mouthfeel? Chocolate can release multiple flavors as it melts. Breathe in, drawing air over your palate to emphasize these tastes.

The most common flavors found in chocolate fall into a number of different categories. They can be **sweet** (honey, vanilla, malt), **bitter** (coffee, hoppy beer, tonic water), **dairy/caramel** (cream, butterscotch, crème brûlée), **fruity** (berry, stone fruit, citrus, jam), **floral** (lavender, rose, tea), **sour** (vinegar, lemon, sour milk), **vegetal** (tobacco, grass, eucalyptus), **earthy** (wood, smoke, mushrooms), **roasted** (toast, nuts, smoke), **spicy** (black pepper, chili pepper, cinnamon), or **chocolaty**, of course (brownie, chocolate pudding, hot cocoa). These are just a few examples to help guide you to the perfect flavor descriptions.

FINISH: Take one more deep breath to help analyze the chocolate's finish. "Finish" describes how long the flavor lasts in your mouth, and the residual experience on your palate, such as mild, harsh, astringent, smooth, spicy, mellow, etc.

chocolate types & percentages

The percentage listed on a chocolate product refers to the amount of cocoa (including cocoa butter) contained within, relative to 100 percent of the ingredients.

Dark, semisweet, bittersweet, and **extra-bitter** are all terms used to describe chocolate that doesn't contain milk. In these types, the remaining weight is made up of sugar combined with other filler ingredients, like vanillin or soy lecithin, which is commonly used in the chocolate industry as a cheap emulsifier. Theo strictly adheres to a formulation of organic cocoa beans, organic sugar, organic cocoa butter, and organic vanilla for our dark chocolate. We never use soy in our products for three important reasons: First, soy doesn't enhance quality. Second, it's a common allergen. Third, most soy contains GMOs, and we decidedly do *not* want GMOs in our food. As a rule, the higher the percentage of chocolate, the less sugar it contains.

Milk chocolate contains milk, so as a rule, it has less cocoa solids than dark chocolate. By law, milk chocolate must contain at least 10 percent cocoa solids (our milk chocolate contains 45 percent, which is more than many dark chocolate formulations currently available).

White chocolate contains cocoa butter, vanilla, and sugar. It contains no cocoa solids other than cocoa butter. Calling it chocolate is a little bit of a misnomer, but it's still quite delicious.

Cocoa powder is 100 percent cocoa solids and therefore contains no sugar. To make cocoa powder, roasted cocoa beans are processed and the cocoa butter is pressed out.

Cocoa nibs are simply the cracked, roasted, shelled cocoa beans. They are made up of the cocoa solid and cocoa butter (or fat) that naturally occur in the cocoa bean.

Chocolate ganache is an emulsion of chocolate and typically milk or cream. Its consistency depends on the amount of liquid it contains. Many of our confections are filled with a stiff ganache that also contains butter for an even smoother mouthfeel, and sometimes we flavor the cream by adding a fruit puree, or by infusing it with herbs or teas.

♥ ♥ ♥

HOW TO STORE CHOCOLATE

Store your chocolate in a cool, dry place, well wrapped, away from strong odors and direct sunlight. Ideally chocolate is stored at an ambient temperature between 65 and 75 degrees F, though once tempered, cocoa butter is a very stable fat as long as it's kept well below 91 degrees F. There is no reason to freeze chocolate, and the only reason to refrigerate it would be if the ambient temperature was climbing towards the 90-degree range.

♥ ♥ ♥

HOW TO MELT CHOCOLATE

Many of the recipes in this book call for melted chocolate. There are two methods you can use, microwave or double boiler (instructions follow), and both require a little bit of care. Whichever method you choose, be sure to **start with finely chopped chocolate and stir frequently**.

It's important not to overheat chocolate, as it can burn fairly easily. As chocolate melts, it maintains its shape, so just looking at it won't tell you if it's melting—you must stir it. When chocolate burns, it becomes granular. If you overheat it, it's easy to mistakenly think that chips and chunks are solid chocolate that has not yet melted, when in fact they are burned bits. If you burn chocolate, you'll have to discard it and start over.

Whenever you work with chocolate, **make sure that all your containers and tools are absolutely dry**. Just one drop of water can cause a bowl of melting chocolate to seize and become very thick and pasty. If this happens, you won't be able to incorporate it evenly into your recipe.

Once your melted chocolate is liquid, smooth, and glossy, proceed with the recipe. If the recipe calls for cooled melted chocolate, set aside, stirring occasionally, until it feels just barely cool to the touch but is still liquid. If the recipe requires that the chocolate be warm, you can reheat it gently just before you use it, if necessary.

Melting Chocolate in a Microwave

Put your chopped chocolate in a microwave-safe bowl and heat it on low power for 10-second increments. Once you've done this a few times and you know your microwave, or if you're working with larger quantities of chocolate (more than 2 ounces), you may warm it for longer just to start, but once the chocolate starts to melt, only heat it for very short intervals. Between intervals, stir the chocolate well. The heat of the melted chocolate is enough to melt some of the solid chocolate that remains. If the container you're using gets warm, continue to stir the melting chocolate, as the heat of the container will melt the chocolate as well.

Melting Chocolate in a Double Boiler

Heat a couple inches of water in a saucepan over low heat. Put the chopped chocolate in a stainless steel or glass bowl large enough to sit securely in the saucepan without touching the water. When the water comes to a simmer, turn off the heat and let the chocolate begin to melt. Stir the chocolate often, and when about two-thirds of it has melted, remove the bowl from the saucepan and dry the bottom of the bowl very well. Continue to stir the chocolate until it has melted completely.

♥ ♥ ♥

HOW TO TEMPER CHOCOLATE AND DIP CONFECTIONS

Tools of the Confectionary Trade

THERMOMETERS

The most important tools at your disposal are your thermometers. Please don't attempt confectionary recipes without them. We suggest investing in both a **candy (or sugar) thermometer** and a **chocolate thermometer**, because a candy thermometer measures a wide range of temperatures and it's difficult to get an exact reading at the low temperatures that chocolate work requires. If you really want to get serious, invest in a **digital probe thermometer** (we use them in our kitchen). It gives a very exact, instantaneous temperature reading. We don't recommend a laser thermometer, as it can give false readings if the laser bounces off the side of a hot pan.

COPPER POTS

If you're going to be making a lot of caramels and brittles, a **heavy unlined** or **tin-lined copper pot** is invaluable. An old-fashioned jam pot is ideal. The next best thing would be a **large, heavy-bottomed pot** that holds around 5 or 6 quarts. A heavy bottom ensures even cooking and decreases the likelihood of sugar burning.

SPATULAS

What did we ever do before silicone spatulas? Rubber spatulas are very useful, but **silicone spatulas** can do everything rubber ones can (there's nothing better for scraping out the very last bit of an ingredient from a measuring cup or folding a delicate batter), and they can do it at very high temperatures. We use them to stir boiling liquids, even boiling sugar, and they're great for scraping down the sides of hot pans.

    Metal offset spatulas (both large and small) are the kind of tools you're sure you'd never use until you have them—then you can't live without them. We use large ones to table temper (see The Table Method, page 30) and spread our confections in their frames. A small offset spatula (with a 3¼-inch blade) is perfect for spreading confections into pans. Use one to push the mixtures into tight corners and smooth the tops like a professional.

We've adapted our confectionary recipes for the home kitchen, to fit in either an **8-by-8-inch** or a **9-by-13-inch pan**. If you have at least one of each of these pans, you're set.

We recommend owning at least one **Silpat baking mat** to use as a pan liner. You can use **parchment paper** instead, but Silpat is ultra-durable, absolutely nonstick, and easy to clean. It makes unmolding caramels a snap. Silpat liners are readily available online or in kitchen stores.

If you're going to temper chocolate and dip confections with any regularity, we recommend buying a **chocolate dipping fork**. There's no need to spend a lot of money, and you can find sets that include a **two-pronged fork**, a **multipronged fork**, and a **swirl** (for dipping round truffles). Of course you can use a regular fork, but dipping forks have long, fine prongs to allow for easier removal of confections than from a regular piece of cutlery.

Tempering Chocolate

In our confection kitchen, we enrobe (or coat) our ganache fillings, caramels, toffees, brittles, and candy bars in tempered, or stabilized, chocolate. The process of tempering is what gives chocolate its shine and snap. When you buy a bar of Theo chocolate, it's in temper, but as soon as you heat it to over 91 degrees F, it's not. We highly recommend tempering your dipping chocolate. If you dip confections in chocolate that's out of temper, the chocolate will fail to set up properly, resulting in too soft a texture, a crumbly mouthfeel, and a dull sheen rather than a glossy shine. You may also see unsightly fat crystals that have separated from the cocoa solid and migrated to the surface, creating streaks or dots.

When melted cocoa butter cools and solidifies, it's actually crystallizing. Those crystals can take six different forms, but only one of those forms (form V, or beta 2 crystals, in case you're wondering) is stable. Once you have a few beta 2 crystals, with enough agitation, they can spread throughout the chocolate and attract others, stacking themselves into extremely stable structures—this is what results in perfectly smooth, shiny chocolate that snaps when you break it. When you temper chocolate, the goal is to convince the cocoa butter to form those very stable beta 2 crystal structures.

tips for successful confectionary work

The most important tips we can offer for successful confectionary work are steps you can take before you even begin a recipe:

· Read through the entire recipe.

· Gather your ingredients together and measure them all out.

· Gather all the equipment you'll need to complete the recipe.

We highly recommend this level of preparation so that you'll be able to focus more on technique and texture once you get going.

To temper, all forms of the chocolate's cocoa butter crystal must be melted (each form melts at a different temperature), to create what we refer to as "blank" chocolate. When the chocolate is blank (there are no crystals), it's cooled to the temperature at which beta 2 crystals form and then rewarmed slightly, just to melt any of the undesirable crystal forms that developed at the lower temperatures. It's key to know that temperature is just one part of tempering. Agitation (stirring or spreading) is crucial because it encourages the beta 2 crystal structures to stack.

TEMPERING THEO CHOCOLATE AT HOME

There are two methods for tempering chocolate at home: the **table method** and the **seeding method**. Both methods require a chocolate thermometer, and the table method also requires a granite or marble slab and two large metal spatulas. We recommend using the seeding method, but will explain both methods so you can try them and decide for yourself. Both sets of instructions will result in 2 pounds of tempered chocolate, ready for dipping, coating, or turning into chocolate bark.

Note that dark chocolate is in temper at about 88 degrees F, milk chocolate at about 86 degrees F, and white chocolate at about 84 degrees F. Once your chocolate is in temper, keep it in a bowl set on a folded kitchen towel to insulate it. If you have an electric heating pad, you can set it to its lowest setting, cover it with a folded towel, and set the bowl on top. If the chocolate starts getting too cool and too thick, you can warm it for 5 or 10 seconds at a time over a double boiler, just until you see the edges starting to melt. Remove the bowl from the heat and stir to blend the chocolate. Check the temperature (make sure it didn't get warmer than 90 degrees F) and check the temper before you use it (see Checking for Temper on page 31).

The table method is the preferred tempering method for professionals. Begin by chopping and then melting 2 pounds of chocolate either in a microwave or a double boiler (see How to Melt Chocolate, page 25, for instructions). Stir the chocolate until it has melted completely, and check that the temperature is about 110 degrees F for dark chocolate, and about 105 degrees F for milk or white chocolate.

Pour about two-thirds of the melted chocolate onto a marble slab. With a large metal spatula in each hand, continuously spread the chocolate across the slab using your dominant hand and then scrape it back up with the same spatula, and wipe that spatula against the edge of the spatula you're holding in your other hand. Move as quickly as you can. As soon as the chocolate begins to thicken, scrape it up and put it back in the bowl with the reserved melted chocolate.

Vigorously stir the bowl of chocolate until it's smooth and check its temperature. You're aiming for between 88 and 90 degrees F. If the chocolate is warmer than that, repeat the tempering until you reach about 90 degrees F. As the chocolate nears temper, you'll notice that if you pull up a spoonful and let it drizzle back into the bowl, it will begin to make a small pile that will sit on the surface of the melted chocolate and slowly sink, rather than immediately pooling. Before you use the chocolate, check that it's in temper.

The Seeding Method

This is the method we teach at the classes we hold at our factory store. It's easy and less messy than the table method, and as long as you're only tempering a couple of pounds at a time, it can be very quick. The idea behind the seeding method is that by introducing already tempered chocolate to blank chocolate, you encourage the growth of beta 2 crystals without lowering the temperature very much. This saves you the effort of cooling and then rewarming the chocolate.

Begin by chopping 2 pounds of chocolate. Set aside about ½ pound. Melt the remaining 1½ pounds chocolate either in a microwave or a double boiler (see How to Melt Chocolate, page 25, for instructions). Stir the chocolate until it has melted completely, and check that the temperature is at least 110 degrees F for dark chocolate, and at about 105 degrees F for milk or white chocolate. Pour the chocolate into a clean bowl (this will help it cool faster), and set it on a kitchen towel to insulate it from the cool counter.

Add 1 tablespoon of the reserved chopped chocolate and stir vigorously until it's completely melted. Repeat once or twice, and then check the temperature of the chocolate in the bowl. You're aiming for between 88 and 90 degrees F for dark chocolate, and 86 to 88 degrees F for milk chocolate. If the chocolate is warmer than that, keep adding the chopped chocolate by the tablespoon and stirring it until it has melted completely, until you reach about 90 degrees F. As the chocolate nears temper, you'll notice that if you pull up a spoonful and let it drizzle back into the bowl, it will begin to make a small pile that will sit on the surface of the melted chocolate and slowly sink, rather than immediately pooling.

Before you use the chocolate, check that it's in temper.

making chocolate bark from leftover chocolate

If you have any leftover tempered chocolate, you can make bark by pouring it onto a piece of parchment paper and sprinkling it with nuts, dried fruit, salt, cocoa nibs, or other toppings. Let it set, break it into pieces, and enjoy!

Checking for Temper

Take a small piece of parchment paper (about 3 inches square) and dip it into the chocolate. Lay the paper flat on your work surface and let the chocolate set. If the chocolate is in temper, within 1 to 2 minutes it will begin to look satiny rather than wet. Within another couple of minutes, it will no longer be tacky and will have a smooth, glossy appearance (no streaks). While you're waiting for the test chocolate to set, continue gently stirring your chocolate.

If the chocolate is far from temper, it will stay wet. If it's close to temper, it may appear to set up, but if you look closely you'll see streaks; if you use the chocolate at this stage, it will develop obvious streaks of white cocoa butter later. If the chocolate is at the right temperature but not setting up correctly, it's not in temper and needs more agitation (not more cooling). In that case, just stir the bowl of chocolate vigorously for 2 minutes and then redo the paper test. Repeat as necessary until the chocolate is in temper.

In order to maintain temper for longer, it's best to set the bowl of tempered chocolate on a kitchen towel for insulation.

Coating with Chocolate

DIPPING GANACHE CONFECTIONS

Once you've completed any of the ganache recipes in Confections (page 185), you might choose to use a melon baller to scoop the fillings, roll them quickly into round truffle shapes, and simply roll them in cocoa powder instead of dipping them in chocolate. But if you choose to dip your confections in tempered chocolate the way we do, here's how.

After you've made the ganache, allow it to set and crystallize at room temperature for a minimum of 12 hours and a maximum of 24 hours. Then lift the block of ganache out of the pan using the excess parchment paper as handles. Turn the block over onto a clean piece of parchment paper set on a cutting board. Melt a little chocolate (this chocolate does not have to be tempered) and spread a very thin layer all over the top of the block of ganache. This coating provides a sturdy base to protect the confection when you pick it up with your dipping fork, and when you fish it out of the dipping chocolate. When the coating has set (you might have to refrigerate the block to help it along), turn the ganache over and use a thin, sharp knife to cut it into squares or rectangles. Run the knife under hot water and dry it between cuts as necessary. Set the ganache pieces on a Silpat mat or parchment paper–lined baking sheet.

Next, temper your chocolate for dipping (see Tempering Chocolate, page 28). Before you begin dipping, it's extremely important to test the temper of your chocolate (see Checking for Temper, page 31). The crystalline structure of chocolate is most unstable just before it reaches temper. If you use it at this stage, it can quickly become covered with streaks and dots of fat crystals that have separated from the cocoa solid.

To dip the confections in chocolate, drop them one at a time, with the chocolate-coated side down, into a bowl of tempered chocolate, then use a dipping fork or round dipping tool to lift them out. (If you can lift them out with part of the confection hanging over the edge of the fork, it will make it easier to remove the dipped chocolate from the fork.)

Gently tap the fork against the edge of the bowl while carefully balancing the confection to let any excess chocolate drip off. Just barely scrape the bottom of the confection along the edge of the bowl to remove the last bit of excess, then place the dipped chocolate on a parchment paper–lined baking sheet.

If you'd like to decorate your confections with a topping such as salt, nuts, spices, or candied flowers, wait about 30 seconds (but not much longer) before applying the decoration to the top of the confection so that it doesn't sink. Let the chocolates set at room temperature for at least 1 hour before handling them. Chocolate-coated ganache confections will keep at room temperature for up to 2 weeks.

DIPPING TOFFEES AND BRITTLES

The easiest way to cover one side of your toffee or brittle with tempered chocolate is to turn the entire, unbroken piece of candy over so that the smooth side is facing up. Use a paper towel to wipe up any buttery sheen that may have formed on the surface. Pour the tempered chocolate over it, covering as much of the candy as possible so that you don't have to spread it very much, and use a small offset spatula to spread it all the way to the edges. (Moving the chocolate around as it cools can cause it to come out of temper.) Let the chocolate set up for about 15 seconds, sprinkle it with toppings, then let the candy set completely before breaking it into pieces.

To completely coat your toffee or brittle with tempered chocolate, wipe off any buttery sheen, break it into pieces, then drop the candy, smooth side down, into the chocolate. Use a dipping fork to turn the candy over, then use the fork to lift it out, scraping the bottom gently against the side of the bowl. Set the candy on a parchment paper–lined baking sheet and sprinkle with toppings, if desired. Be sure to wipe the fork clean between each piece; it will make removing the candy from the fork much easier.

Kept in an airtight container or completely coated with chocolate, toffee and brittle have a shelf life of about 6 weeks. If they are not completely sealed with chocolate or are left uncovered, they tend to get sticky within 1 to 2 days.

DIPPING CANDY BARS

To dip candy, run a small metal offset spatula along the edges of the pan of candy to loosen the contents. Place a piece of parchment paper over the pan and set a cutting board on top. Flip the pan and the cutting board, holding them together tightly, so that the cutting board is on the bottom. Lift off the pan, leaving the candy on the cutting board. Some types of candy will slide out more quickly than others.

Spread a thin layer of tempered chocolate on whichever side of the candy will be the bottom. This coating provides a sturdy base to protect the candy bar when you are coating it with the tempered chocolate.

Once that chocolate layer has set, turn the block of candy over so that the chocolate is on the bottom, and cut it into individual servings with a lightly oiled, sharp long knife. If the knife gets sticky, clean it well before continuing. If you cut the pieces small enough, you can dip them into tempered chocolate as you would dip ganache confections (see Dipping Ganache Confections, page 34). If they are too large to use a dipping fork, the easiest method we've found to use at home involves setting them about 1 inch apart on a cooling rack set over a sheet pan, then slowly ladling tempered chocolate over them. (You won't have to worry about covering the bottoms because they've already been covered with chocolate.) You can scrape up the excess chocolate and either temper it again if it's very clean, or use it in another recipe.

a recipe for nontempered dipping chocolate

We love the snap of tempered chocolate, particularly when it coats a creamy ganache filling. But you may not always want—or have the time—to temper chocolate, and for those occasions, we offer this quick and easy recipe.

MAKES 1 POUND

1 pound Theo chocolate, chopped
3 tablespoons organic extra-virgin coconut oil

- Melt the chocolate and coconut oil together, either in a microwave or in a double boiler (see How to Melt Chocolate, page 25, for instructions). Stir the chocolate while it melts so that it doesn't get too hot.

- When the chocolate has melted, use a rubber or silicone spatula to stir it vigorously and constantly until it's just barely warm. You can transfer the chocolate to a clean bowl to hurry along the cooling process. (If you use it while it's too hot, or without adequately mixing it, the coating won't set well and will remain tacky.) Tap the bowl to release any air bubbles caused by the mixing.

- Dip your confections (see Coating with Chocolate, page 34) and put them on a parchment paper–lined baking sheet to set. Nontempered chocolate takes longer to set than tempered chocolate, but you can put your dipped confections in the refrigerator if you want to speed up the process. Once the coating has set, you can remove the confections from the refrigerator and keep them at room temperature. If you use this recipe to dip any of our candy bars and put them in the refrigerator to set up, be sure to allow them to come to room temperature before serving— caramel, nougat, and marshmallow are hard when they are cold.

chocolate for breakfast

♥ ♥ ♥

Camp Robber Chocolate Raspberry Jam 41

Nibby Butter 42

Preston Hill Bakery Chocolate Bread 43

Nibby Chocolate Granola 47

Fran Costigan's Super-Healthy Nibby Chia Breakfast Sundae 48

Chocolate Pecan Breakfast Rolls 51

Chocolate-Stuffed Crème Brûlée French Toast
with Whipped Cream and Berries 53

CAMP ROBBER CHOCOLATE RASPBERRY JAM

Rome Doherty has been making jam for as long as he can remember. He used to give it away to friends and family until his production got so big they couldn't devour it fast enough. So he began a business he calls Camp Robber Jams, after a little gray bird that's notorious for stealing good food from campsites. Rome sells his jams at Seattle-area farmers' markets and buys as much of his organic fruit as he can from the other vendors. We were honored to find this jam in his lineup and thrilled that he'd share the recipe.

This chocolate-scented jam is particularly lovely on warm scones, brioche, or toast. Just before canning, let a spoonful of the jam cool on a plate and taste it. You can drop in an extra ounce or two of chocolate if you're so inclined. Before you begin, if you aren't already familiar with jam making, review the instructions and make sure you have the necessary equipment (including enough sterilized jars and lids).

MAKES ABOUT 9 HALF PINTS OF JAM

1. Put the raspberries in a large, heavy-bottomed pot and use a potato masher to crush them. Add the pectin, cocoa powder, and lemon juice, and stir thoroughly so that the pectin doesn't clump.

2. Bring the mixture to a boil over medium-high heat, then stir in the sugar. Bring the mixture back up to a full boil and let it boil vigorously for exactly 1 minute. Remove the pot from the heat and let it settle for 5 minutes. Skim any foam that has accumulated, then add the chopped chocolate and let the jam sit for another 2 minutes to melt it. Use a whisk to blend the jam and chocolate until perfectly smooth. Ladle the still-hot jam into sterilized jars, wipe the rims carefully with a clean towel to remove any spills, and screw a lid onto each jar, but don't overtighten.

3. You can process the jars in a water bath, a pressure canner, or the oven. We use a water bath. With a batch this size, it's easiest to do with a real canning pot. If you don't have a canning pot, you can make one by filling your largest pot with water (enough to come up an inch above the jars). Place a folded kitchen towel at the bottom. Bring the water to a full boil. Use tongs to carefully lower the jars so they stand on the towel, cover the pot, and bring it back up to a boil. Boil the jars for 10 minutes (if your boiling water was ready when you finished making the jam, and the jam is still piping hot, you can boil them for 5 minutes). Use tongs to very carefully remove the hot jars from the water, and let them cool to room temperature sitting on a towel. Your jam will keep for 1 year.

½ flat raspberries (6 full half-pint baskets, 2½ to 3 pounds)

⅓ cup (one 1¾-ounce packet) powdered pectin

1 tablespoon cocoa powder

2 to 4 tablespoons freshly squeezed lemon juice (from about 1 large lemon)

7 cups (3 pounds) sugar

3 ounces Theo 85 percent dark chocolate, finely chopped

NIBBY BUTTER

Sometimes (often) simple is best: good butter, cocoa nibs, a crusty baguette. Some of us like this butter with a pinch of salt, and others prefer to start their day with a little something sweeter, so we offer you both options. Either way, add a cup of coffee or tea, and call this an excellent continental breakfast. Serve leftovers later with a glass of red wine, and call it cocktail hour.

MAKES ½ CUP OF BUTTER (THE NUMBER OF SERVINGS DEPENDS ON HOW MUCH YOU LIKE BUTTER)

Savory:

1 tablespoon (¼ ounce) Theo roasted cocoa nibs

½ cup (1 stick) unsalted butter, at room temperature

¼ to ½ teaspoon sea salt

Sweet:

1 tablespoon (¼ ounce) Theo roasted cocoa nibs

½ cup (1 stick) unsalted butter, at room temperature

About 2 teaspoons confectioners' sugar

1. Use a spice grinder or a mortar and pestle to coarsely chop the cocoa nibs. Mix the nibs into the butter using a wooden spoon or the paddle attachment of a stand mixer. Add the salt or confectioners' sugar and blend well. Shape the butter into a log, lay it on a piece of parchment paper or plastic wrap, and roll it tightly. Refrigerate the butter until solid. Slice it and allow the slices to soften slightly at room temperature before serving.

health benefits of cocoa

Ground cocoa is composed of cocoa butter, a natural fat, in which the ground particles of the cocoa seed are suspended. These particles are fibrous and contain a mixture of polyphenols and catechins, antioxidants similar to those in green tea. Dark chocolate with a high percentage of cocoa (like our 70 percent and 85 percent Classic bars) contains a lot of these antioxidants, which have been shown to have positive health benefits, including maintaining healthy blood pressure, inhibiting inflammation, reducing the formation of bacteria known to cause tooth decay, and improving cerebral blood flow. Chocolate also contains theobromine, a mild stimulant related to caffeine.

PRESTON HILL BAKERY CHOCOLATE BREAD

This dark, chewy, intensely bittersweet bread is always among the first to sell out at Preston Hill Bakery's stand at farmers' markets in the Seattle area. Alex Williams is the man who does everything from mixing the doughs and baking the breads to bringing them to market and selling them, and he very kindly shared his recipe with us. We love that Alex uses organic, whole grain flours, and that he bakes his breads in an outdoor wood-fired bread oven he built himself. Alex worked for years as an architect, until he brought his creativity and love of good food to bread baking.

Even though we bake his chocolate bread in a boring old regular oven, it's still stupendous. The perfect accompaniment to a big mug of steaming coffee or a milky latte, it's just as good for breakfast as for a midafternoon or late-night snack. Though stuffed with bits, chunks, and shards of chocolate, the bread itself isn't sweet at all. If it lasts beyond a day or two (which is highly unlikely unless you double the recipe), it makes incredible toast—crispy on the outside, moist and warm inside, and all those bits of chocolate turn molten. Honestly, we have no idea why you're still reading this when you could be baking!

MAKES 2 SMALL (10-OUNCE) LOAVES

1. Put ¾ cup of each bread flour in the bowl of a stand mixer fitted with the dough hook. Stir in the water. Cover and let sit for 45 minutes to activate the gluten.

2. Add the cocoa powder, yeast, and xanthan gum, and mix for about 1 minute at medium speed. Add the salt and mix at medium speed for another minute. Add about a tablespoon of each kind of flour and mix on medium-high speed for about 2 minutes. The dough will be sticky and should form a ball around the hook with almost all the dough. If it doesn't, add another tablespoon of each kind of flour and mix again at medium-high speed for another 2 minutes. Add both chocolates in three additions, mixing for about 30 seconds between additions. If the dough hasn't already come together, it will once you've started adding the chocolate.

3. Transfer the dough to an oiled bowl (it will be sticky—that's OK!), cover the bowl with plastic wrap, and let the dough rise until at least doubled, about 45 minutes.

(continued)

¾ cup plus 2 tablespoons (4 ounces) organic whole wheat bread flour, divided, plus more for dusting

¾ cup plus 2 tablespoons (4 ounces) organic white bread flour, divided

1 cup very warm water

1 tablespoon (¼ ounce) extra-dark cocoa powder

1 teaspoon dry instant yeast

½ teaspoon xanthan gum (see note on following page)

¾ teaspoon kosher salt

3½ ounces Theo 70 percent dark chocolate, chopped unevenly

1¾ ounces Theo 45 percent milk chocolate, chopped unevenly

4. Line a baking sheet with parchment paper. Use a dough scraper or plastic spatula to cut the ball of dough in half. Use the scraper to lift half the dough from the bowl and place it on one side of the baking sheet, tucking it into a ball as much as you can (don't worry too much—even if you can't get it into a neat ball now, it magically bakes up quite beautifully). Repeat with the other half of the dough. Lightly dust the top of the loaves with flour and cover them loosely with a piece of plastic wrap. Let them rise until almost doubled, 30 to 45 minutes.

5. When the dough has almost doubled, preheat the oven to 400 degrees F. Bake the breads for about 30 minutes, until they feel firm and sound hollow when tapped on the bottom, or until the internal temperature reaches 200 degrees F (a probe thermometer works well). Let the breads cool for 5 minutes on the baking sheet, and then transfer them to a wire rack to cool completely.

note: Xanthan gum is usually used as a gluten replacement, but here it improves the texture of the crumb. It can be found in the gluten-free section of most well-stocked supermarkets or purchased online.

NIBBY CHOCOLATE GRANOLA

Just because we put this granola in the breakfast chapter doesn't mean you can't eat it all day long. Of course it would make a fantastic start to your day with milk or your favorite yogurt, but it also makes an excellent snack and a crunchy, chewy, satisfying ice-cream topping.

MAKES ABOUT 10 CUPS OF RIDICULOUSLY GOOD GRANOLA

1. Preheat the oven to 250 degrees F.

2. In a small bowl, stir together the oat bran and water. Set aside. In a large bowl, combine the oats, hazelnuts, coconut, cocoa nibs, brown sugar, and flaxseed. Stir in the oat bran mixture. In a separate small bowl, whisk together the maple syrup, vegetable oil, and salt until smooth. Drizzle it over the oat mixture, and stir well to blend.

3. Spread the granola evenly on a clean half-sheet pan. Bake for about 1 hour and 15 minutes, stirring every 15 minutes, until it feels crispy and toasted, and the edges begin to turn golden.

4. Remove the pan from the oven and sprinkle the apricots and ginger over the granola. Use a metal spatula to fold in the fruit. Sprinkle the chocolate over the hot granola. Let it sit for a minute to melt, then stir in the chocolate.

5. When the pan feels cool to the touch, refrigerate or freeze it just long enough to set the chocolate. Store the granola in an airtight container for up to 3 weeks.

¼ cup oat bran

1 tablespoon water

3 cups old-fashioned rolled oats

1 cup chopped hazelnuts

1 cup unsweetened desiccated coconut

½ cup (2 ounces) Theo roasted cocoa nibs

⅓ cup packed dark brown sugar

2 tablespoons flaxseed

⅓ cup maple syrup

¼ cup vegetable oil

1 teaspoon kosher salt

1 cup finely chopped dried apricots

⅓ cup finely chopped crystallized ginger (optional)

2 ounces Theo 85 percent dark chocolate, very finely chopped

FRAN COSTIGAN'S SUPER-HEALTHY NIBBY CHIA BREAKFAST SUNDAE

This super-healthy, crazy-delicious breakfast sundae comes from Fran Costigan, "the queen of vegan desserts." Fran is an internationally recognized culinary instructor and author, and she's all about making and eating delicious, healthy, organic, and minimally processed food. Naturally, she's also a longtime Theo chocolate devotee.

Fran created this modern version of muesli just for us. Traditionally, muesli is a mixture of uncooked rolled oats, fruit, seeds, and nuts. Invented by a Swiss physician for his patients, it's packed with iron, calcium, zinc, and other important nutrients. Nondairy milk keeps this recipe vegan, and it's also gluten-free if you use certified gluten-free oats. The pudding is rich and creamy but light in texture, and far more interesting than straight chia puddings. Fran also suggests using chocolate-flavored nondairy milk for a Sunday brunch–worthy extra-chocolaty breakfast pudding. This recipe scales up beautifully, so make enough to last a few days.

MAKES 2 SERVINGS

For the pudding:

1 cup nondairy milk (try almond, coconut, hazelnut, oat, or soy)

1 tablespoon black or white chia seeds

⅓ cup old-fashioned rolled oats

1 tablespoon (¼ ounce) Theo roasted cocoa nibs

1 tablespoon maple syrup, plus more if needed

For serving, a selection of:

Berries

Diced fresh fruit

Diced sulfite-free dried fruit

Chopped nuts

Toasted unsweetened shredded coconut

Seeds (such as pumpkin, sesame, hemp, or flax)

Finely chopped 85 percent Theo dark chocolate

1. To make the pudding, pour the nondairy milk into a glass jar or other container with a lid. Sprinkle the chia seeds on top, wait for about 1 minute, then stir with a fork. Set aside for 5 minutes, then stir again.

2. Stir in the oats and cocoa nibs. Cover the jar and refrigerate the pudding for at least 6 hours, preferably overnight, until it's creamy and thickened, stirring a few times if possible. The chia seeds will begin to soften and resemble small tapioca pearls very quickly, but it takes the oats a few hours to become creamy.

3. In the morning, stir in the maple syrup and serve with an assortment of toppings.

4. The pudding can be kept refrigerated for up to 3 days. Stir before eating. If you want to thin it after 1 or 2 days, you can add more nondairy milk.

CHOCOLATE PECAN BREAKFAST ROLLS

We all know that the aroma of hot, yeasty, sweet bread just as it comes out of the oven is irresistible. Now imagine the tender, chewy bite of freshly risen buns mingled with a perfectly balanced, not-too-sweet blend of finely chopped nuts and melted chocolate. Way to start your day!

To enjoy fresh, warm rolls in the morning, you can make the dough, let it rise, fill it and roll it, cut it into buns, and put them on a baking sheet the night before. Cover with plastic wrap and refrigerate them overnight. In the morning, let them come to room temperature while you preheat the oven, then bake. Like magic, you've got hot breakfast buns, even if you slept in.

MAKES 12 ROLLS

1. To make the rolls, in a small bowl, mix the yeast, ¼ cup of the milk, and a pinch of sugar, and set aside.

2. In the bowl of a stand mixer fitted with the paddle attachment, cream together the butter, the remaining ½ cup sugar, the salt, and vanilla on medium speed until light and creamy. Add the yeast mixture, the remaining 1¼ cup milk, and the flours, and mix well on low speed. When all the ingredients have been incorporated, switch to the dough hook and knead on low speed for 3 minutes. The dough will be sticky but will come together in a soft ball around the hook. If it isn't forming a ball, add 1 or 2 tablespoons of flour. Cover the bowl with a piece of plastic wrap and let the dough rise until at least doubled in size, about 2 hours.

3. To make the filling, put the pecans in the bowl of a food processor and pulse until finely chopped (uniform ⅛-inch pieces). Pour the nuts into a small bowl and grind the chocolate in the processor until finely chopped—pieces about the same size as the nuts. Mix the chocolate with the pecans.

4. When you're ready to make the rolls, line a baking sheet with parchment paper and set aside. Turn the dough out onto a lightly floured work surface and gently pat it into a long rectangle. Dust the top with flour and roll the dough out to about 18 inches long and 10 inches wide. Brush the dough with the melted butter, leaving a

(continued)

For the rolls:

1 tablespoon dry instant yeast

1½ cups warm milk, divided

½ cup (3½ ounces) sugar, plus a pinch, divided

½ cup (1 stick) unsalted butter, at cool room temperature

1½ teaspoons kosher salt

1 teaspoon vanilla extract

4 cups (1 pound) all-purpose flour, plus more for dusting

1 cup (5 ounces) whole wheat flour

For the filling:

1 cup pecans, toasted

5 ounces Theo chocolate (we like a mix of 45 percent milk chocolate and 70 percent dark chocolate)

♥ ♥ ♥

2 tablespoons butter, melted

⅓ cup packed light brown sugar

½ cup confectioners' sugar

3 teaspoons milk or half-and-half

1-inch border bare along the long side closest to you. Spread the brown sugar in an even layer over the butter. Sprinkle the chocolate/nut mixture evenly over the sugar. Lightly dust the border with flour.

5. Starting with the edge farthest away from you, roll up the dough toward you, into a log, and leave it sitting on top of its seam. Use a sharp large knife to cut the log in half crosswise, cut each half in half again, and then cut each piece into three. For each roll, unroll just the last inch of dough (the flour you dusted will make this easy), twist the now-loose piece of dough so that you can gently hold it against one of the cut sides of the roll, and set the roll flat on the prepared baking sheet, open-cut-side up (that little flap of dough on the bottom of the roll will help keep the filling inside). Arrange the rolls on the baking sheet in 4 rows of 3, and cover the tray loosely with plastic wrap. At this point, you can refrigerate the rolls overnight for morning baking, or let the dough rise until puffy and about 50 percent larger, about 45 minutes (the time will vary depending on the temperature of your kitchen).

6. Preheat the oven to 350 degrees F. Bake the rolls until they're golden and firm, about 30 minutes. Let them cool on the baking sheet for 10 minutes before icing.

7. To make the icing, whisk the confectioners' sugar and milk together in a small bowl until smooth. Drizzle over the rolls.

CHOCOLATE-STUFFED CRÈME BRÛLÉE FRENCH TOAST WITH WHIPPED CREAM AND BERRIES

When your day starts with chocolate-stuffed anything, you know it's going to be a good one. This decadent French toast was inspired by the one Debra remembers from when she worked at the Old Firehouse, a restaurant in Lanesville, Massachusetts. Folks lined up around the block for it, and we've done our best to do it justice. The Old Firehouse used Portuguese bread, which is a soft, slightly sweet bread. You can make your own, or try to find a loaf; otherwise brioche or challah make very fine substitutes.

While you're cooking, you can put each batch of French toast on a baking sheet in a 250-degree-F oven to keep warm while you make the rest.

MAKES 6 SERVINGS

1. To make the chocolate filling, bring the cream to a boil (it's easiest to heat such a small amount in the microwave) and pour it over the chocolate. Let the mixture sit for 1 minute to melt the chocolate, then stir gently until smooth. Refrigerate the filling to set to a spreadable consistency while you gather the rest of your ingredients.

2. To make the whipped cream, whip the cream and confectioners' sugar to soft peaks and refrigerate until ready to serve.

3. To make the French toast, lay out 6 slices of the bread and spread the filling evenly over all of them. Top each with one of the remaining slices of bread. In a medium bowl, whisk together the milk, eggs, granulated sugar, vanilla, and salt, then pour the custard into a wide, shallow pan such as a 9-by-13-inch baking pan or casserole dish. Place as many sandwiches into the egg mixture as will fit in a large frying pan or on a griddle, and let them soak until soft, about 30 seconds (the soaking time will depend on how soft and fresh your bread is). Turn the sandwiches over (you may have to do this with your fingers) and let the other side soak for another 30 seconds.

(continued)

For the chocolate filling:

¼ cup plus 1 tablespoon heavy cream

5 ounces Theo 70 percent dark chocolate, chopped

For the whipped cream:

1 cup heavy cream

1 tablespoon confectioners' sugar

♥ ♥ ♥

12 (½-inch) slices slightly stale Portuguese bread, brioche, or challah

2 cups whole milk

3 eggs

1 tablespoon granulated sugar

2 teaspoons vanilla extract

¼ teaspoon kosher salt

Butter, for cooking

Turbinado raw sugar, for cooking

3 cups mixed fresh berries, for serving

Pure maple syrup, for serving

4. Heat a frying pan or griddle over medium heat. Add butter to the hot pan, let it melt, and wait for the foam to subside. Lift the sandwiches from the egg mixture and transfer them to the hot pan. Cook until firm and golden on the bottom. Just before you flip them, sprinkle a layer of turbinado sugar on the top of each sandwich—enough so that you can really see the sugar layer—then flip the sandwiches and cook the other side, adding butter if necessary. Make sure the griddle isn't too hot; you want the center of the sandwich to cook without overbrowning the bread. Repeat with the remaining sandwiches, wiping out the pan between batches (you need to remove the excess sugar or it will burn).

5. To serve, place the sandwiches on serving plates, caramelized sugar side up, and serve immediately with the whipped cream, berries, and maple syrup.

on the savory side: small plates

♥ ♥ ♥

CANDIED COCOA NIB AND SOFT CHEESE TOASTS

Chocolate and cheese? Yes! We love pairing chocolate with cheese so much that we offer a frequently sold-out class on the subject at our factory store. These particularly delectable little bites deliver just about everything you could ask for in one nibble: crispy, toasted bread; creamy, savory cheese; and bittersweet, crunchy cocoa nibs. The cheese rounds out the cocoa flavor of the roasted nibs and brings out their natural smoky sweetness.

The candied nibs will keep in an airtight container indefinitely, so the next time you decide on your way home from work to throw an impromptu cocktail hour, all you need to do is pick up a baguette and a piece of cheese (we love to make this with Dinah's Cheese from Kurtwood Farms on Vashon Island, near Seattle), and you've got the makings of a very elegant hors d'oeuvre.

**MAKES 30 TOASTS, WITH EXTRA NIBS FOR SNACKING
(ABOUT 1¼ CUPS CANDIED NIBS IN TOTAL)**

1. Line a baking sheet with a piece of parchment paper and set aside.

2. In a small saucepan over medium heat, spread the sugar in an even layer and let it sit, undisturbed, until about a third of the surface area has melted. Use a heatproof spatula or wooden spoon to gently stir the sugar while the rest of it melts. Keep stirring and cook until the sugar caramelizes and turns a light amber color. Remove the pan from the heat and quickly add the cocoa nibs, butter, and salt. Stir the mixture vigorously to coat the nibs, then pour the mixture onto the prepared baking sheet and spread it out, flattening any clumps, and let it cool completely.

3. Meanwhile, preheat the oven to 450 degrees F. Cut the baguette into ½-inch slices and lay them flat on a baking sheet. Toast them until crisp, about 5 minutes.

4. When the nibs have cooled, use your fingers to break them apart into small bits. To serve, lay thin slices of soft ripened cheese on each toast (or spread the cheese if you're using fresh). Top each toast with about 1 teaspoon of candied nibs, a pinch of the herbs, and a drizzle of the honey.

¼ cup sugar

¾ cup (3 ounces) Theo roasted cocoa nibs

¼ tablespoon unsalted butter

⅛ teaspoon kosher salt

1 baguette

5 to 6 ounces soft ripened or fresh cheese

2 tablespoons finely chopped fresh herbs (such as mint or basil) (optional)

Warm honey (optional)

COCOA-SCENTED DUKKAH

Dukkah is an Egyptian spice blend that's rapidly gaining popularity outside the Middle East; we think it's because the flavor is both exotically aromatic and approachable. There are so many wonderful ways to use it, we made a whole list for you (see following page), which we're sure you'll add to. There are countless *dukkah* recipes circulating, most of which contain nuts, sesame seeds, cumin, and coriander. Of course our version contains our roasted cocoa nibs—because everything tastes better with chocolate.

MAKES ABOUT ¾ CUP SPICE MIX

1. In a small, dry skillet over medium heat, toast the sesame seeds, stirring constantly, until they begin to turn golden. Put them in a small bowl, and set aside to cool.

2. Put the coriander and cumin seeds in the same skillet over medium heat, and toast the spices, moving the pan constantly, until they are fragrant, about 2 minutes. Watch them carefully so they don't burn. Set aside to cool before grinding (don't add them to the sesame seeds yet).

3. When the spices have cooled, coarsely grind them in a small food processor, a coffee or spice grinder, or with a mortar and pestle. Add them to the sesame seeds, along with the hazelnuts, salt, and pepper. Use a small food processor, a mortar and pestle, or a chef's knife to finely chop the cocoa nibs. Add them to the spice mix and stir until well blended.

4. Store the *dukkah* in an airtight container in a cool, dry place. Nuts eventually go rancid, and spices lose their potency, so use this flavorful blend liberally while it's fresh, and try to finish it within 1 or 2 months.

3 tablespoons sesame seeds

1 tablespoon coriander seeds

1 tablespoon cumin seeds

¼ cup hazelnuts, toasted, skinned (if not DuChilly variety—see note), and finely chopped

1 teaspoon kosher salt

¼ teaspoon freshly ground black pepper

⅓ cup (1½ ounces) Theo roasted cocoa nibs

note: You can use any hazelnut variety, but DuChilly hazelnuts, grown in the Northwest, are sweeter and don't need to be skinned. Find them at farmers' markets and online.

(continued)

dukkah-palooza

Here are some of our favorite serving suggestions for *dukkah* to get you started:

- Serve it with crusty bread or grilled pita and olive oil for dipping—first in the oil, then in the spices (couldn't be easier, and this is probably our favorite way to enjoy it).

- Sprinkle it on thick soups such as squash, carrot, or potato leek, before serving.

- Sprinkle it on salads.

- Spread hummus on a serving platter, drizzle it with olive oil, and sprinkle it with *dukkah*, or stir some *dukkah* right into the hummus. Garnish with pomegranate seeds, if desired.

- Roll out pizza dough, brush it with olive oil, sprinkle it with *dukkah*, and bake.

- Dust it on roasted root vegetables.

- Mix it with plain yogurt for a dip or as a sauce for grilled meats.

- Make a topping for crostini by mashing white beans and adding olive oil and *dukkah*.

- Rub portions of fresh salmon or beef fillets with olive oil, roll them in *dukkah* to thoroughly coat, then sear them on both sides.

- Mix ¼ cup *dukkah*, ¼ cup finely chopped hazelnuts, and ¼ cup finely chopped cocoa nibs. Use this to encrust snapper, trout, or any other mild, meaty white fish before pan-frying.

ONION JAM WITH DRIED PLUMS AND CHOCOLATE

Try this wonderfully sticky, dark, and flavorful jam alongside roasted meats such as pot roast, brisket, chicken, duck, turkey, or pork, or on a burger or sandwich. It's also terrific with pâté or a sharp hard cheese such as aged cheddar or *tomme*. It keeps for at least two weeks in the refrigerator, or you can bottle it in cute jars and give it as a gift.

This recipe calls for grappa, an Italian brandy made from the grape seeds, skins, and stems leftover after pressing for wine. As with any ingredient, the better quality grappa you use, the more delicious the jam will be. If you can't find grappa at your local liquor store, you may substitute one-half cup of Madeira or marsala for the one-quarter cup of grappa.

MAKES ABOUT 2¼ CUPS STICKY GOODNESS

1. Preheat the oven to 325 degrees F.

2. In a large, heavy-bottomed ovenproof skillet, melt the butter over medium heat. When the foam subsides, add the onion, shallots, and garlic, and sauté until they're translucent and beginning to turn golden, 8 to 10 minutes. Turn off the heat, and stir in the grappa. The liquid will evaporate almost immediately.

3. Add the plums, coffee, brown sugar, vinegar, cocoa nibs, paprika, salt, and pepper to taste. Mix well. Bring to a simmer, then cover the pan and place it in the oven for 1 hour.

4. After an hour, give the jam a stir. You want there to be only a little liquid left in the pan because the jam will firm up as it cools; if the jam is very wet, replace the lid and put it back in the oven for about 15 minutes.

5. When the jam is ready, stir in the chocolate. Serve at room temperature.

¼ cup (½ stick) unsalted butter

1 pound yellow onions (about 1 large), cut into ¼-inch slices

8 ounces shallots (about 6), cut into ¼-inch slices

1 tablespoon chopped garlic

¼ cup grappa

1 cup chopped dried plums

¾ cup strong freshly brewed coffee

⅓ cup packed light brown sugar

¼ cup sherry vinegar or apple cider vinegar

1 tablespoon (¼ ounce) Theo roasted cocoa nibs, ground

1½ teaspoons smoked paprika

1 teaspoon kosher salt

Freshly ground black pepper

¾ ounce Theo 85 percent dark chocolate, chopped

ZOI ANTONITSAS'S GRILLED ALASKAN SPOT PRAWNS WITH THEO COCOA NIB, ALMOND, AND CHILI PICADA

We've watched executive chef Zoi Antonitsas pour her heart and soul into Seattle hot spot Westward, and her work has more than paid off. Westward is the quintessential locale for a cocktail and oysters, nestled into a little patch of Lake Union shoreline and perfectly appointed with Adirondack chairs, warm blankets, and a fire pit. Once inside, you enjoy a gorgeous Mediterranean-inspired meal. To get a taste of all that nautical goodness, try this garlicky *picada* recipe with prawns.

If you can't get Alaskan spot prawns, you can substitute any good-quality prawns or shrimp. The garlic and red pepper flakes give this wonderfully rough sauce, a staple of Catalan cuisine, a bright bite, but feel free to increase or decrease either or both to taste. Save any leftover sauce to serve with grilled or roasted chicken or pork.

MAKES 4 APPETIZER SERVINGS (3 PRAWNS EACH)

Zest and juice of 1 orange

Zest and juice of 1 lemon

1 cup extra-virgin olive oil, divided

1 teaspoon sea salt

12 very fresh Alaskan spot prawns, shell on, washed and dried

1 cup Marcona almonds, toasted and finely chopped

1 tablespoon finely grated garlic (we recommend using a Microplane)

1 tablespoon finely chopped Italian parsley, plus leaves for garnish

1 teaspoon finely chopped fresh marjoram

1 teaspoon finely chopped fresh thyme

1 teaspoon red pepper flakes

½ cup (2 ounces) Theo roasted cocoa nibs, finely chopped

1 lemon, cut into 4 wedges, for serving

1. In a large nonreactive bowl, whisk together the orange and lemon juices, ¼ cup of the olive oil, and salt. Add the prawns, cover, and marinate in the refrigerator for at least 1 hour, but no longer than 4 hours.

2. To make the *picada*, pour the remaining ¾ cup olive oil into a medium bowl. Add the orange and lemon zest, almonds, garlic, parsley, marjoram, thyme, and red pepper flakes, and stir together. Add the cocoa nibs and taste for salt; if the almonds were salted, you may not need to add any at all. Set the *picada* aside to let the flavors meld while you ready the grill and cook the shrimp.

3. Heat a grill to medium-high. Remove the prawns from the marinade. Grill them for about 90 seconds on each side, just until cooked through—don't overcook them. Put the hot prawns in a bowl, add half of the *picada*, and toss to coat them with the sauce.

4. To serve, stack 3 prawns on each plate. Top with some of the remaining *picada*. Garnish with a lemon wedge and a couple of parsley leaves.

MIXED GREENS WITH MUSHROOMS AND NIBS

We like to toss our roasted cocoa nibs into salads for a healthy crunch packed with antioxidants. Their flavor goes so well with earthy mushrooms, slightly bitter greens, and the caramel notes of aged cheese that we'd venture to say this is a match made in salad heaven.

These instructions are for a cold salad, but you can also try this dish warm; just add the mushrooms to the dressing while they're still hot, and toss the salad together right away. The cheese will begin to melt and the leaves will wilt a little. And just like that, you've made a hearty, filling salad that's perfect for a cool day.

MAKES 4 TO 6 SIDE SALADS

4 tablespoons extra-virgin olive oil, divided

7 or 8 medium cremini or button mushrooms, cut into ¼-inch slices

½ teaspoon kosher salt, divided, plus more for seasoning

1 tablespoon sherry vinegar, plus more if needed

Freshly ground black pepper

1½ tablespoons Theo roasted cocoa nibs

6 cups mixed baby greens

Generous ½ cup shredded aged Gouda cheese

1. Heat 2 tablespoons of the olive oil in a large frying pan over medium-high heat. Add the mushrooms and ¼ teaspoon of the salt, and sauté the mushrooms until golden brown, about 5 minutes. Set aside to cool.

2. Meanwhile, in a large bowl, whisk together the remaining 2 tablespoons oil and ¼ teaspoon salt, the vinegar, and pepper to taste. Add the sautéed mushrooms, cocoa nibs, and greens, and toss to mix. Add the cheese and toss to coat the leaves with dressing and evenly distribute all the ingredients. Taste a leaf and add salt, pepper, and vinegar to taste.

NIBBY CRACKERS

We know, who really takes the time to make crackers? But this is another one of our all-time favorite recipes and totally worth the effort. These crackers are perfectly crunchy, a little bit sweet, and a little bit spicy, with roasted cocoa overtones from the cocoa nibs. When we make them at our factory, team members line up to take some home. They pair very well with cheese and wine, and keep for up to two weeks in an airtight container, so don't hesitate to double the recipe. We serve these at our popular chocolate-and-cheese pairing classes and get so many requests for the recipe that we hand it out after class.

MAKES ABOUT 5 DOZEN SMALL (1½-INCH) CRACKERS

1. Preheat the oven to 375 degrees F. Line a baking sheet with a piece of parchment paper and set aside.

2. In a medium bowl, whisk together the flour, sugar, baking powder, chili, and salt.

3. In a measuring cup, combine the wine and olive oil, then pour the liquid ingredients into the dry ingredients and mix with a spoon until the dough begins to come together. Add the cocoa nibs and gently knead the dough until they're evenly distributed and the dough is smooth. Cover the dough with a piece of plastic wrap and set aside to rest for about 10 minutes.

4. On a lightly floured surface, roll the dough out to ⅛-inch thickness. Use a long knife to trim the edges (or not, it's up to you) and then cut the dough into small (1½-inch) squares or diamonds. If you trimmed the edges, gather the scraps of dough into a ball, roll it out, and cut it into more crackers.

5. Transfer the crackers to the prepared baking sheet (they won't spread, so you can place them close together). Use a fork to prick each cracker a few times. Bake the crackers until they're firm and golden brown, 18 to 20 minutes. Transfer the baking sheet to a wire rack and let the crackers cool completely before storing them in an airtight container.

1 cup (4½ ounces) unbleached white bread flour (or all-purpose flour in a pinch)

¼ cup (1¾ ounces) sugar

1½ teaspoons baking powder

1 teaspoon ground pasilla chili (or other mild to medium chili)

½ teaspoon kosher salt

¼ cup dry red wine

3 tablespoons extra-virgin olive oil

2 tablespoons (½ ounce) Theo roasted cocoa nibs, chopped

chocolate tasting & pairing parties

Pairing chocolate with other food or drink is an easy, fun, and delicious launch pad for a party. We love pairing Theo chocolate with wine, beer, or cheese and offer classes on the topic throughout the year at our factory store. We also make a pairing kit for both beer and wine that includes instructions and an assortment of chocolates to get you started. Since there's already a lot of information out there about pairing chocolate with wine, here are some guidelines for pairing it with beer and cheese.

When pairing any kind of food and drink, two major flavor strategies apply: complement or contrast the flavors. However, a successful pairing is any pairing you like, and the possibilities are endless.

♥ ♥ ♥

Getting Your Party Started

- Break the chocolates into small pieces and serve them, labeled, on separate plates so your guests can try your pairings or make their own.

- Offer at least three different kinds of beer or cheese.

- Set out palate cleansers such as water crackers or slices of plain baguette, and room temperature water.

- Provide paper and pens for taking notes.

♥ ♥ ♥

Beer and Chocolate

Beer's low alcohol content makes its flavor very prominent. There isn't that burn that you encounter when tasting spirits or some wines, making it easier to pick out specific flavors.

Carbonation is another unique component to beer. It helps refresh your palate not only from the flavor of the chocolate but also from the cocoa butter that may coat your mouth during tasting.

When choosing beer for a tasting, pick at least three with different flavors and mouth-feel to help create distinct and exciting pairings. You can start with a selection of beers from your favorite local brewery or one you've never heard of. You can also try beers of similar styles from different breweries and compare them, or just grab a selection of bottles that look interesting. Just remember, there are no wrong answers—a successful pairing is one that you like.

TYPES OF BEER PAIRINGS TO TRY

- **Stouts** and **porters** are some of the darkest beers. They are rich and medium- to full-bodied with assertive malt flavors and pair well with spicy chocolates, such as our **Chili** or **Coconut Curry bars**, and with rich dark chocolates, such as our **Coffee bar**.

- **Pale**, **blond**, and **wheat ales** pair well with our **Orange bar**. The bright citrus complements the natural clean fruitiness of these beer types.

- **Strong winter ales** are rich and smooth with dominant malt flavors. They pair well with our **85 percent dark chocolate**, **Congo Vanilla Nib**, or **Coconut Curry bars**.

- **Hoppy beers** impart fruity, citrusy, floral notes without overwhelming bitterness. They pair beautifully with all kinds of chocolate. Try our **Chili**, **Coconut Curry**, or **Orange bars**.

When you're tasting beer, pour it into a glass so you can see its color, clarity, and head. Swirl the beer to aerate it: oxygen stimulates carbonation and makes the beer smell and taste more vibrant. Smell it—all complex flavors are greatly impacted by scent. When you taste the beer, think about its body, texture, and flavor; you can use the same vocabulary you'd use for wine or chocolate (see How to Taste Chocolate, page 22) to describe the flavors. After you swallow, breathe in deeply to draw air over your palate. This accentuates the aftertaste of the beer.

There are more than two hundred craft breweries in Washington State, and since 2006 we've had the only state-legislated beer commission in the country. The Washington Beer Commission holds craft beer festivals throughout the year. We've enjoyed taking part in many of them, pairing our chocolate with beer, and we're proud to count among our customers a long list of award-winning breweries that use our cocoa nibs to flavor their beers, including **Deschutes Brewery**, **Georgetown Brewing Company**, **Elysian Brewing Company**, and **Old Schoolhouse Brewery**.

♥ ♥ ♥

Cheese and Chocolate

The creamy texture and earthy flavors of cheese pair remarkably well with chocolate. Milder, creamy cheeses call for high-percentage milk chocolate, while bolder-flavored hard cheeses usually pair better with darker, more intense chocolate.

ABOUT THE CHEESEMAKERS WE'VE HIGHLIGHTED FOR PAIRING OPTIONS:

Since 2002, **Beecher's Handmade Cheese** has been entrenched in the Seattle food scene. They handcraft their cheeses in a glass-enclosed facility at Seattle's Pike Place Market so customers can learn how they're made. Beecher's uses only locally produced fresh milk that's rBST- and antibiotic-free. In 2011, they opened a second location in New York City's Flatiron District and began selling cheese made with milk from herds just south of the state's capital of Albany.

Mt. Townsend Creamery handcrafts their cheeses in Port Townsend, on the Olympic Peninsula northwest of Seattle, using high-quality milk from a single herd of cows at a family-owned dairy farm in Sequim, Washington. Inspired by the region's cheesemaking heritage, owners Matt Day and Ryan Trail started Mt. Townsend Creamery in 2005 with the goal of making cheeses "with a sense of place," by using old-world methods to produce artisan varieties.

TYPES OF CHEESE PAIRINGS TO TRY

- **Theo Ghost Chili Caramel** with **Beecher's Flagship**
  Flagship is dense and creamy, with hints of browned butter and caramel. Our caramel brings out the cheese's natural sweetness, and the ghost chili's slow burn echoes the sharpness that comes from Flagship's aging. Also try making a grilled cheese sandwich with this cheese and our 70 percent dark chocolate; for a peppery note, add some arugula leaves.

- **Theo Orange** with **Beecher's No Woman**
  The fruitiness of our Orange bar complements the slightly sweet and spicy Jamaican jerk spices in this complex, smoky, and earthy cheese.

- **Theo Sea Salt** with **Beecher's Marco Polo**

  This creamy cheese is studded with lightly milled green and black peppercorns. Pair it with our salted dark chocolate bar for a quirky twist on the classic salt and pepper. We like to make a fondue by melting 1 pound of the chocolate with ¼ cup heavy cream over low heat and stirring until smooth. Serve with sticks of the cheese and a selection of fruit (dried and fresh) for dipping.

- **Theo Hazelnut Crunch** with **Beecher's Dutch Hollow Dulcet**

  Our milk chocolate brings out the cheese's creaminess, which in turn highlights the crunch and sea salt in the chocolate. This cheese has a delicate flavor that would be overpowered by a dark chocolate.

- **Theo Pure 45 Percent Milk Chocolate** with **Mt. Townsend New Moon Washington Jack**

  This rich, creamy chocolate brings out New Moon's buttery, slightly sweet flavor and subtle butterscotch undertones.

- **Theo Coconut Curry** with **Mt. Townsend Red Alder Toma**

  Toasted coconut enhances the nutty characteristics of this natural-rind, Alpine-style cheese (which is hand-washed and aged) and the curry spices pair well with its earthy flavors.

- **Theo Fig, Fennel & Almond** with **Mt. Townsend Cirrus Pacific Northwest Camembert**

  Savory fennel pairs well with this strong cheese, and the sweet fig and chocolate are pleasantly opposing flavors.

- **Theo Ginger** with **Mt. Townsend Seastack**

  This cheese ripens from the outside—the ripened areas develop an earthy, garlic flavor, while the less ripe interior maintains a bright citrus taste. Our warming, sweetly spicy ginger chocolate complements both flavors.

ROASTED BABY CARROTS WITH BALSAMIC—BITTER CHOCOLATE SYRUP

Real baby carrots, the kind with lacy green tops and delicate peel (as opposed to the factory-shaped cylindrical ones that come in a bag), are tender and sweet and practically worth the trip to the farmers' market just for them alone. They're so delicious they don't really need anything at all. But hey, sometimes we like to gild the lily, and as much as we honor the perfection that is the real baby carrot, this surprisingly simple syrup steals the show here, elevating an already perfect vegetable into an elegant, dramatic, delectable side dish. The syrup goes equally well with roasted beets, and it's also sublime drizzled over a well-seasoned grilled steak. Let your imagination run wild with this sauce—it will enliven a wide range of dishes.

MAKES 6 TO 8 SIDE-DISH SERVINGS

1. Preheat the oven to 375 degrees F.

2. Put the carrots on a sheet pan, drizzle them with the olive oil, and spread them in a single layer. Sprinkle the salt evenly over the carrots, and lay the thyme sprigs on top. Roast until the carrots are tender and brown in spots, shaking the pan and turning once or twice, about 35 minutes total.

3. While the carrots are cooking, make the syrup. Put the vinegar in the smallest saucepan you have and simmer over medium-low heat until reduced to ¼ cup. Remove the pan from the heat and add the chocolate. Let the chocolate melt for 30 seconds, then use a small spatula to gently stir the syrup until the chocolate has melted completely and the syrup is smooth. Add the honey and salt and mix well. Cover the pan to keep the sauce warm until you're ready to serve the carrots.

4. To serve, discard the thyme and arrange the carrots on a serving dish. Drizzle them generously with the syrup, and serve immediately.

3 pounds baby carrots (about finger-width thick), green tops trimmed to about 1 inch

3 tablespoons extra-virgin olive oil

1½ teaspoons kosher salt

5 or 6 (4-inch) sprigs fresh thyme

For the syrup:

½ cup aged balsamic vinegar (5- or 10-year aged is fine)

½ ounce Theo 85 percent dark chocolate, chopped

½ teaspoon honey

Generous pinch kosher salt

ROASTED SQUASH WITH BROWN BUTTER NIBS

We especially love exploring textures at Theo, and this easy recipe combines the melt-in-your-mouth tenderness of roasted squash with the gentle crunch of cocoa nibs. It will work with any of your favorite winter squash, such as butternut, acorn, delicata, or kabocha. Just be sure to roast your squash long enough to achieve a truly soft texture. The brown sugar will help it caramelize, and the nutty brown butter and nibs plant this dish squarely under the heading of comfort food.

MAKES 4 TO 8 SIDE-DISH SERVINGS

1 winter squash (about 2 pounds), halved and seeded

1 tablespoon extra-virgin olive oil

1 tablespoon firmly packed dark brown sugar

1 teaspoon kosher salt

2 tablespoons unsalted butter

1 generous tablespoon (about ¼ ounce) Theo roasted cocoa nibs

1. Preheat the oven to 400 degrees F.

2. If using butternut squash, cut it into 1½-inch pieces. Cut acorn squash into 8 wedges. Cut delicata into ½-inch-thick half-moons. Leave kabocha in halves. Rub the cut squash with the olive oil, sprinkle with the brown sugar and salt, and place the pieces in a roasting dish or on a sheet pan. Roast until the squash is tender and the edges are nicely browned, about 30 minutes. If using butternut, stir once or twice while cooking. If using delicata, turn the pieces over after 20 minutes.

3. When the squash is tender, melt the butter in a small saucepan over medium heat. Continue to cook until the foam subsides, you start to see brown specks at the bottom of the pan, and the butter smells nutty. Add the cocoa nibs and cook for 10 seconds just to warm them through, then spoon the mixture over the squash and serve immediately.

STRAWBERRY SALAD WITH LACY NIB COOKIES

We admit that this salad is a bit of a guilty pleasure—after all, there are cookies in it!—but we're firm believers that chocolate has a place in the center of the plate. We love the contrast of the sweet, crunchy cookies with the sharp dressing, tender strawberries, and tangy goat cheese. Note that this recipe makes a lot of Lacy Nibs, but any fewer and the batter would be too difficult to mix. They're so delicious though, you'll be glad to have extra to snack on. This dish would be supersweet for a special Valentine's Day meal.

The cookies tend to get soft and chewy in just a few hours, so rather than baking more than you need, store the leftover batter in the refrigerator for up to one week and bake the cookies for snacking or for salad as you need them.

MAKES 4 SIDE SALADS AND A WHOLE LOT OF COOKIES

1. To make the cookies, preheat the oven to 400 degrees F. Line a baking sheet with parchment paper and set aside.

2. In the bowl of a stand mixer fitted with the paddle attachment, cream the butter and brown sugar together on medium speed until smooth. Scrape down the sides of the bowl, add the milk, and blend until smooth. Add the flour, cocoa powder, and salt, and mix well. Fold in the cocoa nibs.

3. Using a ½ teaspoon measuring spoon (yes, so tiny!) drop the batter onto the prepared baking sheet, 3 inches apart. Bake until the entire surface of each cookie is bubbling, about 7 minutes. It's perfectly fine if they run together—you can snap them into smaller shards for serving. Let the cookies cool completely before removing them from the parchment paper.

4. To make the salad, in a large bowl whisk together the vinegar, shallot, honey, salt, and pepper to taste. Whisk in the olive oil. Add the greens and toss to coat the leaves with dressing. Add the strawberries and toss again.

5. To serve, divide the salad among 4 small plates. Top each salad with a quarter of the goat cheese and 3 of the cookies. Serve immediately.

For the cookies:

3½ tablespoons unsalted butter, at room temperature

½ cup packed (3½ ounces) dark brown sugar

2 tablespoons whole milk

1 tablespoon all-purpose flour

1½ teaspoons cocoa powder

¼ teaspoon kosher salt

½ cup (2 ounces) Theo roasted cocoa nibs

♥ ♥ ♥

1 tablespoon raspberry vinegar

1½ teaspoons finely minced shallot

1½ teaspoons honey

⅛ teaspoon kosher salt

Freshly ground black pepper

2 tablespoons extra-virgin olive oil

6 cups mixed greens

1 cup sliced strawberries

2 ounces crumbled fresh goat cheese

chocolate for dinner

♥ ♥ ♥

Honey- and Saffron-Braised Chicken
with Cocoa Nib Couscous 82

Naomi Pomeroy's Theo Chocolate Mole Sauce 84

Pumpkin-Filled Chocolate Ravioli with
Sage Brown Butter, Pears, and Hazelnuts 86

Tilth's Toasted Durum Tagliatelle with Lamb Sugo 89

Tom Douglas's Roast Chicken and Wild Mushroom
Warm Bread Salad with Cocoa Nibs 91

HONEY- AND SAFFRON-BRAISED CHICKEN WITH COCOA NIB COUSCOUS

This wonderfully warming braise was inspired by our Honey Saffron Caramel. Sure to become one of your go-to dishes, it's quick to put together and can be left alone during its forty-five-minute simmer, making it perfect for a weeknight supper. The honey helps the onions caramelize perfectly, and cooking the couscous in the braising liquid with cocoa nibs gives it so much flavor that it's hard to believe such complexity can come from so few ingredients.

MAKES 6 SERVINGS

3 cups chicken stock

½ teaspoon packed saffron (about 1 teaspoon loosely mounded)

2 tablespoons extra-virgin olive oil

6 bone-in, skin-on chicken thighs (about 2½ pounds)

Kosher salt and freshly ground black pepper

2 medium onions, thinly sliced

1 tablespoon minced garlic

3 tablespoons honey, divided

½ cup dry white wine

4 large carrots, cut into ¼-inch slices

1 (14-ounce) can diced tomatoes

2 cups couscous

2 tablespoons (½ ounce) Theo roasted cocoa nibs, finely ground

¼ cup pitted green olives, halved

1. In a medium saucepan over medium-low heat, bring the chicken stock to a simmer. Turn off the heat and add the saffron. Cover the pan and set aside to let the saffron steep.

2. In a heavy-bottomed pot large enough to hold all the chicken thighs in one layer, heat the olive oil over medium-high heat. Season the chicken on both sides with salt and pepper to taste, and brown the pieces, skin side first, for 3 to 5 minutes per side. Place the chicken on a plate and set aside.

3. Add the onions to the pot along with a few pinches of pepper, and sauté them, over medium heat, until they're limp and translucent, about 5 minutes. Turn down the heat if they start to brown before they're soft. Add the garlic and 2 tablespoons of the honey, and sauté, stirring occasionally, until the onions are golden brown, about another 5 minutes. Add the wine and simmer for about 1 minute. Add the carrots, tomatoes, and saffron-infused stock and bring to a boil. Replace the chicken, tucking the pieces into an even layer, and reduce the heat to low. Cover the pot tightly and simmer gently for 45 minutes.

4. After 45 minutes, remove the chicken from the pot. Ladle 3 cups of the cooking liquid from the pot into a small saucepan (about 2½ quarts works well) and bring it to a boil. Immediately stir in the couscous and cocoa nibs, then turn off the heat and cover the pan.

5. If there's more than an inch of liquid remaining on top of the onions, simmer to reduce the sauce. When the sauce has thickened slightly, add the olives and replace the chicken. Drizzle with the remaining 1 tablespoon honey. Cover the pot and cook on low just to warm the chicken.

6. To serve, fluff the couscous with a fork. Put a mound of couscous on each plate and top with a chicken thigh. Taste the sauce and season with salt and pepper to taste. Ladle a generous serving of the sauce and vegetables over the chicken and serve immediately.

NAOMI POMEROY'S THEO CHOCOLATE MOLE SAUCE

Naomi Pomeroy is one of the most talented and sassiest women we know in the food world. She's not only the rock star chef-owner of Beast in Portland, Oregon, and winner of a 2014 James Beard Award for Best Chef Northwest (along with a host of other accolades), but she's also the mama bear to a girl we adore named August, and a longtime Theo supporter. Naomi's recipe is definitely one of the more challenging recipes in this book—but (wo)man, is it worth the effort!

Mexican mole sauces always involve a long list of ingredients. Traditionally they were prepared by hand, and the work was shared by many women. A spice grinder and a blender lighten the load, but still, making mole is better as a rainy day activity than a quick supper, unless you prepare the sauce or even just the paste ahead of time and freeze it. When you're ready to use the paste, thaw it and fry it in a little fresh oil, then add your stock, sugar, salt, and chocolate.

Naomi recommends setting aside each part of the ingredient list as you prepare it so you can double-check that you've used everything. She also suggests investing in a candy/deep-fry thermometer (indispensable for many recipes in this cookbook) to be sure that you're frying at 350 degrees F.

It's traditional to simmer turkey in mole, but you can also use chicken or pork, and Naomi also recommends a hard squash such as butternut. Serve it with rice, quick-pickled red onion, and chopped cilantro.

MAKES 9 TO 10 CUPS OF SIMMERING SAUCE

For the spice mixture:

½ cinnamon stick

5 black peppercorns

1 clove

⅛ teaspoon anise seeds

⅛ teaspoon cumin seeds

2 dried avocado leaves (available at well-stocked Latin American grocers)

⅛ teaspoon dried thyme

⅛ teaspoon dried Mexican oregano (available at Latin American grocers, or substitute Mediterranean oregano)

1. Preheat the oven to 350 degrees F.

2. While the oven is heating, make the spice mixture. In a small, heavy-bottomed skillet (such as cast iron), toast the cinnamon stick, peppercorns, clove, and anise and cumin seeds, shaking the pan often, until lightly fragrant. Let the spices cool, then grind them into a fine powder along with the avocado leaves, thyme, and oregano in a small food processor, a coffee or spice grinder, or—as a last resort— with a mortar and pestle. Set the spice mixture aside in a small dish.

3. Spread the pumpkin seeds out in one quarter of a sheet pan, the sunflower seeds in the next quarter, the pecans in the third quarter, and the peanuts in the final quarter. Toast until fragrant and light golden—the pumpkin seeds will take 8 to 10 minutes, then remove them from the sheet pan and continue toasting the rest. The sunflower seeds will take another 3 to 5 minutes, and the nuts will take another couple of minutes. Don't let them burn or your mole will be bitter. Set the toasted seeds and nuts aside in a small dish.

4. Increase the oven temperature to 450 degrees F. Put the tomatoes on a clean sheet pan and roast them until the skin is peeling away and turning brown, and the tomatoes are very soft, about 30 minutes. Let them cool until you can handle them, then peel, seed, and chop them, and set aside.

5. For frying, line another sheet pan with several layers of paper towels and set aside. In a 6- to 8-quart heavy-bottomed pot, heat the canola oil to 350 degrees F as measured on a deep-fry thermometer. Fry the pasilla, ancho, and guajillo chilies until they puff and darken slightly, about 30 seconds. Use a slotted spoon or a basket strainer to quickly remove them from the oil to the prepared sheet pan to drain. Next, fry the plantains until dark golden, 3 to 5 minutes, and remove them to drain on the sheet pan. Fry the onions until blistered and golden brown, about 5 minutes, and remove them to drain on the sheet pan. Fry the brioche until toasted—this happens quickly and you'll want to turn the bread once to toast it evenly. Next, fry the garlic, just until blistered and golden, about 30 seconds. Don't let the garlic burn or it will taste very bitter. Make sure that everything you fry turns a dark-golden color in order to develop the complex flavors that make mole so wonderful, and be sure to let the oil come back up to temperature between each batch. Reserve about 3 tablespoons of the frying oil in a small bowl.

6. In a blender, puree some of the spice mixture, seed-nut mixture, tomatoes, and fried ingredients with some of the prunes and a little stock. Just add enough stock to get the blender moving. Blend until the paste is smooth, then transfer it to a clean bowl. Repeat in batches until all the ingredients have been blended.

7. Once you've pureed all the prepared ingredients, in a large, heavy-bottomed pot, heat the reserved frying oil over medium heat. Add the mole paste and cook, stirring, until it's hot and slightly darker in color. Stir constantly so it doesn't burn. Add the remaining stock (more or less, depending on how thick you want the sauce) and mix well. Stir in the sugar, then the salt, and finally the chocolate. Taste the sauce for seasoning and add more sugar and/or salt to taste.

♥ ♥ ♥

2 tablespoons pumpkin seeds (also called *pepitas*)

¼ cup raw sunflower seeds

2 tablespoons pecan pieces

2 tablespoons skin-on peanuts

2 large tomatoes (about 12 ounces)

3 cups canola oil

4 dried pasilla chilies, stemmed and seeded

2 dried ancho chilies, stemmed and seeded

2 dried guajillo chilies, stemmed and seeded

1 ripe plantain, cut into ½-inch slices

½ medium onion, cut into ½-inch slices and separated into petals

2 slices brioche or challah bread

2 large or 3 small cloves garlic

¼ cup chopped prunes

1½ quarts (6 cups) chicken or vegetable stock

3 tablespoons packed *muscovado* or dark brown sugar

½ teaspoon kosher salt

2¼ ounces Theo 85 percent dark chocolate, chopped

PUMPKIN-FILLED CHOCOLATE RAVIOLI WITH SAGE BROWN BUTTER, PEARS, AND HAZELNUTS

All the flavors of fall come together in this elegant pasta dish. The pumpkin- and ricotta-filled ravioli are a gorgeous cocoa color and very satisfying. You can make the ravioli ahead of time and freeze them on parchment paper–lined baking sheets, then store them in a freezer bag until you want to cook them. The sauce comes together very quickly, so be sure to have your ingredients prepped before you start boiling the ravioli.

MAKES 6 TO 8 SERVINGS

For the dough:

5 eggs

1 ounce Theo 85 percent dark chocolate, melted (see page 25)

2½ cups all-purpose flour, plus more as needed

For the filling:

1 tablespoon extra-virgin olive oil

¼ cup finely chopped shallots

1 cup ricotta cheese

1 cup pumpkin puree

¾ teaspoon kosher salt

⅛ teaspoon ground cinnamon

Generous pinch ground allspice

Generous pinch ground cloves

For the sauce:

½ cup plus 2 tablespoons (1¼ sticks) unsalted butter

1 pear, cored and cut into ½-inch dice

12 large fresh sage leaves, cut into thin ribbons (chiffonade)

Kosher salt

1. You can make the pasta dough either in a stand mixer or by hand. To use a stand mixer, fit it with the whisk attachment and whisk the eggs together to break them up, then add the melted chocolate and whisk to break up again. The mixture won't be smooth, but don't worry.

2. Whisk in 1½ cups of the flour on medium speed until blended, then switch to the dough hook attachment. Add the remaining 1 cup flour and mix on medium-low speed until a smooth ball of dough forms around the hook, adding more flour if necessary. Mix on low speed to knead the dough for about 3 minutes. When the dough is smooth and firm, wrap it in plastic wrap and let it rest in the refrigerator for at least 1 hour.

3. To make the pasta dough by hand, put the flour in a bowl and make a well in the center. In a separate bowl, whisk together the eggs and the melted chocolate to break them up. Pour the egg mixture into the well. Use a fork to incorporate the flour into the egg, bit by bit. When most of the flour has been incorporated, knead the dough, adding more flour as needed, until it's smooth and firm, 10 to 15 minutes. Wrap the dough in plastic wrap and let it rest in the refrigerator for at least 1 hour.

4. To make the filling, in a small sauté pan over medium heat, heat the olive oil. Add the shallots and sauté until soft and translucent, about 2 minutes. In a medium bowl, thoroughly combine the cooked shallots, ricotta, pumpkin, salt, cinnamon, allspice, and cloves. Set the filling aside.

5. To make the ravioli, line a baking sheet with parchment paper and set aside. Cut a slice of the pasta dough (leave the dough you're not working with wrapped in plastic wrap) and flour it well. Using a pasta machine, roll it into a thin sheet (less than 1/16 inch thick—number 5 on most pasta machines). Cut the sheet across into rectangles about 2 inches wide and 5 inches long. Place 2 teaspoons of filling about 3/4 inch from one end of each rectangle. Lightly brush water around the filling, then fold the dough to enclose the filling. Press to seal the edges. Fill the ravioli quickly, before the dough dries out. Set the filled ravioli on the prepared baking sheet. Repeat with the remaining dough. When you've filled the baking sheet, cover the filled ravioli with another sheet of parchment paper, and set the next batch of finished ravioli on top. Refrigerate or freeze the ravioli until you're ready to cook them.

6. To make the sauce, bring a large pot of salted water to a boil for the ravioli. While it's coming to the boil, melt the butter in a medium saucepan over medium heat. Continue cooking the butter until the milk solids have turned brown and the butter is caramel-colored and smells nutty. Turn off the heat and add the pear and sage. Stir to combine the ingredients and stop the butter from cooking. Season with salt to taste. Cover the pan and set aside to keep the sauce warm while you cook the ravioli.

7. Boil the ravioli in batches until tender, about 10 minutes (cooking time will depend on how thick you rolled the dough and whether you're cooking them fresh or frozen) and drain.

8. To serve, divide the ravioli among serving plates. Top them with the sauce and sprinkle with the hazelnuts, cocoa nibs, and some cheese. Serve immediately.

For serving:

1/3 cup hazelnuts, toasted, skinned (if not DuChilly variety—see note, page 61), and chopped

1 1/2 tablespoons (1/3 ounce) Theo roasted cocoa nibs

Freshly grated Parmigiano-Reggiano cheese

TILTH'S TOASTED DURUM TAGLIATELLE WITH LAMB SUGO

Maria Hines is a James Beard Award–winning chef with three certified-organic (and much loved) restaurants in Seattle. She has also been a friend since we first started Theo, and we love her for her dedication to using organic, local, sustainable ingredients, as well as her amazing spirit and warmth. This soulful dish comes from Jason Brzozowy, chef de cuisine at her first and widely lauded restaurant, Tilth.

You can make the tagliatelle ahead of time. Refrigerate it, well dusted with durum and wrapped in plastic wrap, overnight. Or freeze it loose on the sheet pan you used to collect the noodles, then carefully transfer the noodles to an airtight container or freezer bag for storage. Cook them from frozen; just add an extra minute or two to your cooking time.

The *sugo*, an Italian meat sauce, can also be made ahead, but don't add the cherry tomatoes and fresh herbs until just before you're ready to serve it.

MAKES 6 TO 8 SERVINGS

1. To make the pasta dough, preheat the oven to 350 degrees F. Spread the durum flour on a sheet pan and toast it until it's just beginning to turn beige (from yellow) and has a nutty aroma, about 20 minutes. Set aside to cool completely.

2. In the bowl of a stand mixer fitted with the dough hook, mix the cooled durum flour, type "OO" flour, cocoa nibs, and olive oil on low speed for 3 minutes. Add the whole eggs and the egg yolk. Drizzle in just enough water to make the dough hold together when you squeeze it (probably between ¼ cup and ½ cup). Once the dough comes together, continue to mix on low speed for 5 minutes. Wrap the dough tightly in plastic wrap and let it rest in the refrigerator for at least 2 hours or overnight.

3. About 1 hour before you want to roll out the pasta, remove the dough from the refrigerator and let it come to room temperature. Cut the dough into quarters. Using a pasta machine, roll the dough into sheets less than ⅟₁₆ inch thick (number 5 on most pasta machines). Cut the sheets into tagliatelle (strips about ½ inch wide). The easiest way to do this is to dust half the length of the rolled pasta with semolina and fold the other half over it. Then dust half the length

(continued)

For the pasta dough:

1 cup plus 2 tablespoons (7⅛ ounces) fine durum wheat flour (semolina), plus more for dusting

1¾ cups (8¾ ounces) type "OO" flour (available from specialty grocers or online)

1½ teaspoons Theo roasted cocoa nibs, coarsely ground

1 teaspoon extra-virgin olive oil

3 eggs

1 egg yolk

About ½ cup water

For the lamb sugo:

2 tablespoons canola oil

2 pounds ground lamb

1 medium onion, minced

4 garlic cloves, minced

2 tablespoons tomato paste

1 cup dry red wine

1 quart (4 cups) chicken stock

1 pound heirloom tomatoes, cored and roughly chopped

3 tablespoons (¾ ounce) Theo roasted cocoa nibs

Kosher salt and freshly ground black pepper

1 pound cherry tomatoes, halved

2 tablespoons chopped fresh oregano, plus more for serving (optional)

1 tablespoon chopped fresh mint, plus more for serving (optional)

♥ ♥ ♥

Freshly grated Parmigiano-Reggiano cheese, for serving

Finely grated Theo 85 percent dark chocolate, for serving

again and fold the rest over that. Continue dusting and folding until you have a little packet no more than 4 or 5 inches long. Then use a heavy, sharp knife to cut strips. Unravel each strip onto a sheet pan dusted with semolina and set the pasta aside until you're ready to cook it. (You can also refrigerate or freeze the noodles for later use; see the headnote.)

4. To make the *sugo*, heat the canola oil in a wide, heavy-bottomed pan over medium-high heat. Add the lamb and brown it, breaking it into pieces with the back of a spoon. Remove the lamb from the pan and drain the excess fat, reserving 2 tablespoons. Put the reserved fat back into the pan and add the onion and garlic. Sauté over medium heat until the onions are translucent and the liquid has evaporated, 3 to 5 minutes. Add the tomato paste and stir to incorporate, then add the wine to deglaze the pan, scraping the bottom of the pan to remove any bits of browned meat or vegetable. Continue cooking to reduce the wine by half, 2 to 3 minutes.

5. Return the browned meat to the pan, and add the chicken stock, heirloom tomatoes, and cocoa nibs. Simmer the *sugo*, uncovered, until the sauce has thickened, about 45 minutes. Season to taste with salt and pepper.

6. To serve, bring a large pot of salted water to a boil. Add the pasta and cook until al dente, about 3 minutes. Drain the pasta. Add the cherry tomatoes, oregano, and mint to the *sugo* and stir to incorporate. Add the drained pasta. Serve the pasta and *sugo* in individual bowls topped with Parmigiano-Reggiano, chocolate, and herbs.

TOM DOUGLAS'S ROAST CHICKEN AND WILD MUSHROOM WARM BREAD SALAD WITH COCOA NIBS

You really can't talk about food in Seattle without mentioning legendary restaurateur Tom Douglas. Tom has been a Theo supporter since the very early days of our factory, and we are forever grateful to him and his CEO, Pam Hinckley, for their influence on our company. Tom is larger than life, and so is this recipe!

Introducing your new favorite roast chicken recipe, à la Tommy D: the sweet raisiny heat of Aleppo pepper and the earthy, roasted flavor of cocoa nibs permeates the moist meat of the chicken. The toasted bread soaks up the chicken juices, tender caramelized mushrooms add an earthy richness, and a little bit of vinegar and peppery fresh arugula brighten the dish. Although there may seem to be a lot of steps when you read through the recipe, they're simple and the preparation is well worth the effort.

MAKES 4 SERVINGS

1. To make the chicken, preheat the oven to 425 degrees F. In a small bowl, combine the butter and ground cocoa nibs. Season to taste with Aleppo pepper and salt (start with about 1 teaspoon of pepper for a mild flavor; add more if you prefer your chicken spicy).

2. Use your fingers to loosen the skin of the chicken over the breast, then spread the flavored butter under the skin. Season the skin of the chicken with more salt and black pepper to taste. Put the lemon, thyme, and whole cocoa nibs in the chicken's cavity, and put the chicken on a rack in a roasting pan.

3. Roast the chicken, basting occasionally, until the juices run clear and a meat thermometer inserted in the thickest part of the thigh reads 175 degrees F, 50 minutes to 1 hour.

4. While the chicken is roasting, start the bread salad. Trim the top and bottom crusts from the bread; leave some of the side crust attached. Cut the bread into 4 thick slices. Brush both sides of each slice with olive oil and brown both sides in a hot grill pan or sauté pan. Tear the toasted bread into irregular chunks and put them in a large ovenproof serving dish with the apricots and nuts.

(continued)

2 tablespoons unsalted butter, softened at room temperature

1 teaspoon Theo roasted cocoa nibs, ground, plus 2 teaspoons whole nibs, divided

Aleppo pepper

Sea salt

1 chicken (about 3½ pounds), trimmed of excess fat, cavity cleaned, rinsed, and patted dry

Freshly ground black pepper

¼ lemon

A few sprigs fresh thyme

For the bread salad:

½ loaf rustic bread

¼ cup extra-virgin olive oil, plus more for brushing

5 dried apricots, finely diced

1½ tablespoons pine nuts, toasted

1½ tablespoons red wine vinegar

Kosher salt and freshly
ground black pepper

1 pound assorted wild
mushrooms, cleaned,
trimmed, and sliced

A few handfuls of arugula or
other greens

1 tablespoon (¼ ounce) Theo
roasted cocoa nibs

5. Make a vinaigrette by whisking together the vinegar and olive oil in a small bowl. Drizzle half of the vinaigrette over the bread and season with salt and pepper to taste. Reserve the remaining vinaigrette and set the bread aside.

6. When the chicken is cooked, remove it from the oven. Lift the chicken from the roasting pan and set aside to rest on a rimmed sheet pan or some other dish that will hold any juices that run out. Put the mushrooms in the hot roasting pan and return the pan to the oven. Roast the mushrooms until tender and caramelized, stirring once or twice, 15 to 20 minutes. About 5 minutes before the mushrooms are ready, put the dish of bread salad in the oven to warm.

7. When the mushrooms are ready, remove both the roasting pan and the bread salad from the oven. Add the mushrooms to the bread salad, along with a couple tablespoons of the juices collected from the resting chicken, and toss together. Add the arugula and the remaining vinaigrette, season to taste with salt and pepper, and toss to combine. Sprinkle the salad with the cocoa nibs.

8. To serve, carve the chicken and place the pieces on the bread salad. Serve immediately.

cookies & bars

♥ ♥ ♥

THEO CHOCOLATE CHUNK BROWNIES

Some of us describe the flavors in our 70 percent dark chocolate as reminiscent of rich, fudgy brownies, so creating this incredibly simple brownie recipe was a no-brainer. You'll be amazed at the flavor and silky texture achieved with so few ingredients—it's literally our favorite brownie recipe in the whole wide world of brownie recipes. Once you've become as attached to it as we are, you might want to try using our Classic Orange, Mint, Chili, or Raspberry 70 percent dark chocolate bars for a simple flavor twist. Around the winter holidays, try making them with our 70 percent Peppermint Stick bars.

MAKES 16 BROWNIES

12 ounces Theo 70 percent dark chocolate, chopped, divided

¾ cup (5¼ ounces) granulated sugar

¼ cup packed (1¾ ounces) light brown sugar

½ cup (1 stick) unsalted butter

⅔ cup (3 ounces) all-purpose flour

½ teaspoon kosher salt

3 eggs

½ teaspoon vanilla extract

1. Preheat the oven to 375 degrees F. Line an 8-inch square baking pan with parchment paper or aluminum foil, leaving a small overhang to facilitate removing the finished brownies. Butter the lining or spray it with nonstick cooking spray, and set the pan aside.

2. Melt 8 ounces of the chocolate in a double boiler along with the sugars and butter, stirring occasionally, (see Melting Chocolate in a Double Boiler, page 26, for instructions), and set aside to cool slightly. Sift the flour and salt together into a small bowl and set aside.

3. Whisk the eggs into the warm chocolate mixture one at a time until thoroughly combined, then whisk in the vanilla. Gently stir in the dry ingredients in two batches, then stir in the remaining 4 ounces chopped chocolate. Pour the batter into the prepared pan and bake for about 20 minutes, or until a toothpick inserted in the center comes out with moist crumbs attached, but not wet with raw batter.

4. Cool completely before cutting, if you can wait that long! These are also delicious served chilled.

a note on measurements

Most of the dry ingredients for baking recipes have been measured in both volume and weight for your convenience. Note that measurements in ounces/grams refer to weight, not volume.

CHOCOLATE CHILI CHURROS

Chocolate dates back to the ancient tribes of Mexico and Central America, who mixed ground cocoa with spices in a hot drink. Flash forward and everything old is new again—our Chili 70 percent dark chocolate bar flies off the shelves, and our Ghost Chili Caramels (page 201) are among our most popular. If you're a heat seeker, use your favorite dried chili in these fudgy versions of the Mexican classic. Try ancho, cayenne, and habanero, or chipotle, if you like a smoky flavor. If heat's not your thing, use a mild chili such as poblano, or omit the spice entirely.

Churros are easy to make, but they can be a little tricky to fry; the oil really needs to be right at 375 degrees F. If it gets too cold, the churros will fall apart. On the other hand, if the oil gets too hot, the outside of the churros will get crispy, but the insides will remain raw. When they're cooked properly, the outside gets wonderfully crisp and the inside stays moist and creamy.

MAKES ABOUT 1 DOZEN 4-INCH CHURROS

1. To make the churros, sift the flour, cocoa powder, and chili together in a small bowl, and set it next to the stove. In a medium saucepan over medium heat, bring the water, butter, sugar, and salt to a boil, stirring to dissolve the sugar and salt. Stir in the dry ingredients quickly and vigorously. Continue to stir over medium heat until the dough comes together in a buttery ball, about 2 minutes. Take the pan off the heat and let the dough cool slightly.

2. Meanwhile, heat 2 inches of vegetable oil in a wide (at least 9 or 10 inches) pot over medium heat. Have a deep-fry thermometer ready. Fit a large piping bag (or a heavy-duty resealable plastic bag with a corner snipped off) with a ½-inch star tip (a closed star tip will make the shape of the churros more well-defined, but any large star tip will work). In a wide, shallow bowl or a cake or brownie pan, stir together the sugar and cinnamon and set it next to the stove.

3. When the oil reaches about 325 degrees F, transfer the batter to the piping bag. When the oil reaches 375 degrees F, squeeze 4-inch lengths of batter into the oil. Do this in batches—don't overcrowd the pot or the oil temperature will drop. Try to release the batter just a few inches above the oil so it doesn't splash and burn you; you can cut the batter with a knife to release each churro, or use a pair of scissors. Fry the churros for 2 to 3 minutes, turning them at least once and moving them gently with a slotted spoon so they don't stick to the bottom. Use the slotted spoon to remove them from the oil and immediately roll them in the cinnamon sugar. Check the temperature of the oil before frying the next batch. Serve the churros as soon as you've fried all the batter.

⅔ cup (3 ounces) all-purpose flour

¼ cup plus 1 tablespoon (1 ounce) cocoa powder

½ teaspoon ground dried chili (as hot or mild as you like)

1 cup water

¼ cup (½ stick) unsalted butter, cut into pieces

1 tablespoon plus 2 teaspoons (¾ ounce) sugar

¼ teaspoon kosher salt

Vegetable oil, for frying

For the cinnamon sugar:

¾ cup sugar

1 tablespoon plus 2 teaspoons ground cinnamon

ALMOND–OLIVE OIL SABLÉ COOKIES WITH CHOCOLATE

Our Salted Almond 45 percent milk chocolate bar, packed with crunchy almonds and just the right amount of salt, is one of our favorite Theo Classic bars. It's hard to beat the salty-sweet satisfaction it delivers. Inspired by those bars, these melt-in-your-mouth cookies are rolled in almonds for extra flavor and crunch, and finished with sea salt before baking. Try making extra rolls of dough to keep in the freezer. Ideally, thaw the dough overnight in the refrigerator, but in a pinch, let it sit on the counter for 15 minutes while the oven preheats, then use a chef's knife to slice it. The smaller you chop the chocolate, the easier it will be to slice the dough.

MAKES ABOUT 4 DOZEN COOKIES

1 cup (4½ ounces) all-purpose flour

⅔ cup (3 ounces) cake flour

½ cup (2 ounces) almond meal

½ teaspoon fine sea salt

½ cup plus 2 tablespoons (1¼ sticks) unsalted butter, at room temperature

3 tablespoons fruity extra-virgin olive oil

¾ cup (3⅓ ounces) confectioners' sugar

1 egg yolk

¼ teaspoon almond extract (optional)

2 ounces Theo 70 percent dark chocolate, chopped

½ cup sliced almonds, finely chopped

Fleur de sel or other flaked sea salt (such as Jacobsen Salt Co.'s Pure Flake), for sprinkling

1. In a medium bowl, whisk together both flours, the almond meal, and salt, and set aside.

2. In the bowl of a stand mixer fitted with the paddle attachment, cream the butter on medium speed until smooth, about 2 minutes. With the mixer running, slowly add the olive oil, stopping once to scrape down the sides of the bowl, until completely blended. Mix in the confectioners' sugar, then add the egg yolk and almond extract and mix on medium speed. Add the dry ingredients and the chocolate and mix on low speed to combine.

3. Turn the dough out onto a lightly floured surface and form it into a log about 16 inches long and 1½ inches in diameter (the dough will be a little sticky). Spread the almonds out on the surface and gently roll the dough over the nuts, pressing to adhere. Continue rolling and gently pressing until the surface of the log is coated with the nuts. Wrap the log in plastic wrap or parchment paper and carefully transfer it to the refrigerator for at least 2 hours or overnight. (You can also freeze the dough at this point for later use.)

4. When you're ready to bake the cookies, preheat the oven to 400 degrees F. Line 2 baking sheets with parchment paper. Cut the log of dough into ¼-inch-thick slices and place them at least 1 inch apart on the prepared sheets. Top each cookie with a pinch of *fleur de sel*.

5. Bake the baking sheets one at a time in the center of the oven for 10 to 12 minutes, or until the edges of the cookies are golden. Watch them carefully, as they burn easily. Cool the cookies on a wire rack and store them in an airtight container. They will keep for at least 4 days.

HAZELNUT MACARONS WITH GIANDUJA GANACHE

Long adored in parts of Europe, *macarons* seem to have made it across the pond and are now all the rage. There's something both endearing and elegant about these cookies, and they offer a very winning combination of satisfying flavor and texture. They're usually made with ground almonds, but our version uses hazelnuts because we fill them with *gianduja*, a heavenly concoction of freshly ground hazelnut butter and our rich milk chocolate.

Ideally, these cookies are made with aged egg whites. To age your whites, simply separate your eggs a day or two before you make the cookies. Put the whites in a container, cover them with plastic wrap, poke a few holes in the plastic to let them dry out a little, and keep them refrigerated. Be sure to let them come to room temperature before you use them. The other trick to these cookies is to make them a day before you plan to serve them: their crisp shells will absorb moisture from the filling, making them extra moist and chewy.

MAKES ABOUT 3 DOZEN FILLED COOKIES

1. Preheat the oven to 250 degrees F. Line 2 baking sheets with parchment paper and set aside.

2. Spread the hazelnut meal on a third baking sheet. When the oven is hot, bake the meal for 30 minutes to dry it out. Set aside to cool.

3. When the hazelnut meal has cooled, put it in the bowl of a food processor, add the confectioners' sugar, and grind for about 1 minute, stopping to pulse 2 or 3 times to get what's climbing the sides to fall. Check that the meal isn't clumping, then grind again for another minute, pulsing 2 or 3 times. Sift the mixture through a fine mesh strainer. If there's more than a tablespoon of nut meal left in the strainer, grind this portion again. If there's less than a tablespoon left, just discard it.

4. In the bowl of a stand mixer fitted with the whisk attachment, whisk the egg whites on medium speed until completely frothy. Gradually add the granulated sugar while the mixer is running. When all the sugar has been added, increase the speed to medium-high and whip the whites until they're stiff and glossy.

5. Take the mixing bowl off the stand mixer, add half the hazelnut mixture to the egg whites, and, using a spatula, fold them together. Add the remaining hazelnut mixture and fold together until completely mixed. The batter will be very stiff. You want to continue folding it until the batter softens and drips off your spatula in a long ribbon, rather than falling off in clumps. A drop of batter should take about 30 to 45 seconds to reincorporate into the rest of the mixture.

2 cups (7 ounces) ground hazelnut meal

2 cups (9 ounces) confectioners' sugar

4 egg whites, at room temperature

½ cup (3½ ounces) granulated sugar

For the filling:

¾ cup hazelnuts, toasted and skinned (if not DuChilly variety—see note, page 61)

4 ounces Theo 45 percent milk chocolate, melted (see page 25)

¼ cup heavy cream

(continued)

6. Scrape the batter into a piping bag (or a heavy duty resealable plastic bag with a corner snipped off) fitted with a ½-inch round tip. Pipe 1-inch kisses of batter at least 1 inch apart onto the prepared baking sheets. Hold the bag perpendicular to the baking sheet with the tip about ½ inch off the surface of the paper. Squeeze out a bit of batter, and stop squeezing before you lift the bag away. This will keep the kiss flat—you want the tail you leave behind to be as small as possible.

7. When you've filled the first baking sheet, tap it firmly on the countertop to flatten the tails and release any air bubbles trapped inside. Repeat with the second baking sheet.

8. Leave the baking sheets on the countertop, uncovered, until a skin forms on top of the cookies, about 30 to 60 minutes depending on the temperature and humidity of your kitchen. While the cookies are resting, adjust the oven racks to the top and bottom thirds of the oven, and preheat it to 280 degrees F.

9. To bake, place 1 baking sheet on each rack and bake for 7 minutes. Rotate the pans top to bottom and front to back, and bake for about another 7 minutes. The *macarons* will have developed a "foot" on the bottom, and be smooth and slightly shiny with no cracks. You can remove a pan from the oven to see if they will lift from the parchment, or just gently press on a cookie—if it barely moves or doesn't move on its foot, it's ready. If in doubt, bake for another minute.

10. Let the cookies cool completely on the baking sheets while you make the ganache filling.

11. To make the filling, grind the hazelnuts in a food processor until they become hazelnut butter (it won't be perfectly smooth, but that's OK). Transfer the butter to a medium bowl, add the chocolate, and stir to blend. Add the cream and stir to incorporate. If the filling is very liquid, let it sit at room temperature until spreadable.

12. When the cookies are cool, turn half of them upside down. Put a teaspoon of filling on each of the upside-down cookies. Place another cookie on top, and gently press them together (it's easiest to almost screw them together) until the filling spreads all the way out to the edge.

13. Cover the *macarons* and refrigerate for 24 hours. Bring them back to room temperature before serving.

CHOCOLATE-SWIRL MERINGUES

These crispy, crunchy, melt-in-your-mouth morsels are all about contrast. Both the intense flavor and color of the dark chocolate swirl really pop against the sweet white meringue. Don't be afraid to sandwich some ganache between two of these for an extra special cookie-like creation.

Our meringue recipe is traditional, with a Theo twist, of course. We like the flavor and texture that result from this ratio of egg white to sugar, but the batter is so thick it can be difficult to make the chocolate swirl. We add a little water to make it easier to work with, and any excess water evaporates in the oven.

MAKES ABOUT THIRTY 2-INCH COOKIES

1. Adjust the oven racks to the top and bottom thirds of the oven, and preheat it to 250 degrees F. Line 2 baking sheets with parchment paper and set aside.

2. In the bowl of a stand mixer fitted with the whisk attachment on medium speed, whip the egg whites, cream of tartar, and salt until foamy. Increase the speed to high and continue whipping the mixture until it holds stiff peaks. Slowly add the sugar, about ¼ cup at a time, whipping for at least 30 seconds between additions. Continue whipping until the meringue is smooth and glossy. Put a little of the batter on your index finger and rub it together with your thumb to check that the sugar has dissolved. Add the water and vanilla, and whisk for 30 seconds, or until completely blended.

3. Drizzle some of the melted chocolate over the top of the batter in thin lines, close together. (We use a small piping bag made of parchment paper and cut just a tiny bit of the paper from the tip to make a small hole.)

4. To shape the meringues, use a dessert spoon to cut across the lines of chocolate (rather than with them), scooping about ½ inch deep into the batter, until you've filled the spoon. Use another spoon to scrape the batter onto the prepared baking sheets, lifting and twisting the spoons to make the chocolate lines swirl. Place the meringues at least 2 inches apart.

(continued)

3 egg whites

¼ teaspoon cream of tartar

Pinch of kosher salt

1 cup (7 ounces) sugar

1 tablespoon water

1 teaspoon vanilla extract

2 ounces Theo 85 percent dark chocolate, melted (see page 25)

5. When you've scooped up the top layer of batter, drizzle more of the chocolate on top of the remaining batter, and then scoop cookies from that layer. Repeat until you've used up all the chocolate and all the batter.

6. You can bake both sheets of cookies at the same time, for about 1 hour 10 minutes, or until they lift easily from the parchment. Because the oven temperature is so low, you can remove one cookie from the oven and set aside to cool for a few minutes. When it's cool, check that it is baked to your liking. If you like your meringues drier, just bake them for a little longer.

COCONUT CURRY–MILK CHOCOLATE BISCOTTI

If you can't tell already, we like to keep things interesting. When we first started Theo, we set out to shake up the chocolate category. Our Coconut Curry 45 percent milk chocolate bar was one of our first products, and it certainly achieved our goal, acquiring a cult following to this day and quickly landing us on Oprah's Favorite Things list!

Our impulse to keep things interesting persists with this biscotti recipe. We are masterful at successfully combining unexpected flavors (like our Ghost Chili Caramels, page 201), and these super-crunchy cookies are no exception. The curry lends a savory note but isn't overpowering, and the combination of curry with nutty coconut makes these wonderfully aromatic. Sweet milk chocolate rounds out the flavors and guarantees the addictiveness of these exotic treats.

MAKES ABOUT 2 DOZEN COOKIES

2½ cups (11¼ ounces) all-purpose flour

1½ teaspoons baking powder

1 teaspoon kosher salt

½ cup (1 stick) unsalted butter

1 cup (7 ounces) sugar

1 teaspoon curry powder

3 eggs

1¼ cups shredded unsweetened coconut

6 ounces Theo 45 percent milk chocolate, chopped

1. Preheat the oven to 350 degrees F. Line a baking sheet with parchment paper and set aside.

2. In a small bowl, whisk together the flour, baking powder, and salt, and set aside.

3. In the bowl of a stand mixer fitted with the paddle attachment, cream the butter and sugar on medium-high speed until smooth and fluffy, 3 to 5 minutes. Use a rubber spatula to scrape the bowl. Add the curry powder and blend well. Add the eggs, one at a time, mixing well to incorporate each egg before you add the next one, and scraping the bowl between additions. Add the coconut and chocolate and mix well. Add the dry ingredients and mix on low speed to combine.

4. On the prepared baking sheet, form the dough into a 15-by-3-inch log, then flatten the log with your palm or fingertips to about 1½ inches thick. Bake for about 1 hour, until the log is golden brown and firm to the touch. Set the baking sheet on a wire rack and let the log cool until it's cool enough to handle, about 30 minutes.

5. Carefully transfer the log to a cutting board. Use a large, heavy knife to cut it into ¾-inch-thick slices. Place the slices cut side down back on the baking sheet (they'll have to be very close together). Bake them for 10 minutes, then turn them over and bake for another 10 minutes. Let the biscotti cool completely before serving. Store them in an airtight container for up to 1 week.

GOOEY DOUBLE-CHOCOLATE MOCHA COOKIES

Attention, serious chocolate devotees: this recipe is for you! Extremely chocolaty, tender, and fudgy, these cookies are the ultimate treat for a real chocolate lover. The result is so good that in 2012 the recipe was a winner of the CNN Fair Trade Chocolate Challenge, which invited people to develop recipes using Fair Trade ingredients.

If coffee isn't your thing, feel free to leave it out, and be sure to try the variations that follow.

MAKES ABOUT 2 DOZEN COOKIES

10 ounces Theo 70 percent dark chocolate, chopped, divided

¼ cup (½ stick) unsalted butter

⅓ cup (1½ ounces) all-purpose flour

¼ teaspoon kosher salt

¼ teaspoon baking powder

1 tablespoon finely ground Fair Trade coffee beans

2 eggs, at room temperature

¾ cup (5½ ounces) sugar

1 teaspoon vanilla extract

1 cup chopped walnuts, toasted (optional)

1. Preheat the oven to 350 degrees F. Line 2 baking sheets with parchment paper and set aside.

2. Melt 7 ounces of the chocolate with the butter in a double boiler (see Melting Chocolate in a Double Boiler, page 26) and set aside to cool slightly.

3. Sift the flour, salt, and baking powder together into a small bowl, stir in the coffee, and set the bowl aside.

4. In the bowl of a stand mixer fitted with the whisk attachment (or in a bowl with a whisk by hand), whip the eggs and sugar together on medium speed until very thick and pale, 3 to 4 minutes (about 8 minutes by hand). Add the vanilla and mix well. Fold in the cooled chocolate mixture, then the dry ingredients, and finally the remaining 3 ounces chopped chocolate and the walnuts.

5. Use 2 spoons or a small cookie scoop to drop rounded tablespoons of batter 2 inches apart onto the prepared baking sheets. Bake the cookies, one sheet at a time, until they're puffed, shiny, and cracked, 8 to 10 minutes. Let the cookies cool completely on the baking sheet—they will be very fragile.

give these variations a try!

♥ ♥ ♥

GOOEY CHOCOLATE MINT COOKIES

Substitute our Mint 70 percent dark chocolate for all 10 ounces of the dark chocolate, omit the coffee and walnuts, and fold in 3 ounces of chopped 45 percent milk chocolate instead of the dark chocolate at the end.

GOOEY CHOCOLATE GINGER COOKIES

Substitute our Ginger 70 percent dark chocolate for all 10 ounces of the dark chocolate, omit the coffee and walnuts, and fold in ½ cup (2½ ounces) finely chopped crystallized ginger at the end.

HELLO ROBIN'S MACKLES'MORES

This cookie was created by Robin Wehl Martin, owner of Hello Robin, to honor Seattleite Macklemore, the rapping half of musical artists Macklemore and Ryan Lewis. Martin's little cookie shop on Seattle's Capitol Hill is the kind of place every neighborhood should have. It's a really happy place, bursting with warmth and personality, and a constant stream of decadent treats like this one coming out of the oven. Martin tops these cookies with half a square of Theo chocolate, but feel free to use a whole square.

MAKES 3 DOZEN COOKIES

1. Line 2 baking sheets with parchment paper and set aside. In a medium bowl, whisk together the flour, cinnamon, baking soda, and salt, and set the bowl aside.

2. In the bowl of a stand mixer fitted with the paddle attachment, cream together the butter and both sugars on medium-high speed until pale and fluffy, about 3 minutes. Add the eggs, one at a time, mixing on medium speed for 15 seconds after each addition. Add the vanilla and mix until smooth. Add the dry ingredients and mix until combined. Fold in the dark chocolate chunks and marshmallows.

3. Using a medium cookie scoop (about 1½ tablespoons), scoop the dough into balls, and put them close together on one of the prepared baking sheets. Freeze the dough for at least 1 hour.

4. When you're almost ready to bake, preheat the oven to 400 degrees F, and put the graham crackers side by side on the second prepared baking sheet.

5. When the dough is frozen and the oven is hot, put 1 ball of cookie dough on each graham cracker, and bake until puffed and just turning golden, 10 to 12 minutes. Remove the pan from the oven and immediately press 1 piece of milk chocolate onto each hot cookie. Be sure to really press the chocolate into the soft cookie so when it melts, it puddles on the cookie and doesn't run off. (For an extra-rich cookie, you can use a whole square of chocolate.)

6. Try to let the cookies cool for a few minutes before you eat them—they're just about as messy to eat as a real fireside s'more!

2¾ cups (12½ ounces) all-purpose flour

1 teaspoon ground cinnamon

1 teaspoon baking soda

1 teaspoon kosher salt

¾ cup (1½ sticks) unsalted butter

1 cup packed (7 ounces) light brown sugar

½ cup (3½ ounces) granulated sugar

2 large eggs

1 teaspoon vanilla extract

4 ounces Theo 70 percent dark chocolate, cut into chunks

1 cup packed mini marshmallows

1 recipe Theo Graham Crackers (recipe follows) or 36 store-bought graham crackers

7½ ounces Theo 45 percent milk chocolate, each square of chocolate halved

(continued)

theo graham crackers

We're betting that these are the best graham crackers you'll ever eat. In addition to using them as the base for Hello Robin's Mackles'mores, you can also enjoy them just as they are or in classic s'mores. For a gluten-free variation, see the recipe that follows. If you love these crackers, try our Big Daddy Marshmallow Bars (page 209). The graham cracker crust is made with the same dough.

MAKES 3½ DOZEN GRAHAM CRACKERS

3¼ cups (15 ounces) all-purpose flour

1⅓ cup plus 2 tablespoons (8 ounces) graham flour

¾ cup (5½ ounces) sugar

1½ teaspoons baking soda

1 teaspoon kosher salt

1¼ cup (2½ sticks) plus 3 tablespoons cold unsalted butter, cut into ½-inch pieces

⅔ cup honey

2 tablespoons molasses

- Preheat the oven to 350 degrees F. Line 2 baking sheets with parchment paper and set aside.

- Put both flours, the sugar, baking soda, and salt in the bowl of a food processor. Pulse a few times until well blended. Add the butter and pulse until the mixture resembles cornmeal.

- In a small bowl, stir together the honey and molasses. Add this mixture to the bowl of the food processor and process until completely mixed and no streaks of honey remain.

- Turn the dough out onto a lightly floured work surface. Separate the dough into 2 portions and form each into a smooth ball. Roll each ball out to about ⅛ inch thick. Use a long knife to cut the rolled-out dough into 2½-inch squares. Combine the scraps to roll the dough out again, repeating the cutting instructions.

- Place the squares of dough about 1 inch apart on the baking sheets. Use a fork to prick each square 3 to 4 times.

- Bake the crackers, 1 sheet at a time, until deep golden brown, about 18 minutes. Cool the crackers on a wire rack.

theo gluten-free graham crackers

S'mores for everyone! In the summer, we celebrate s'mores days at our factory store in Fremont. We fire up a couple of grills and set out a veritable buffet of s'mores ingredients (peanut butter cups! coconut! dark chocolate! our Coffee & Cream bar!), and then we toast marshmallows as fast as we possibly can. You should see the looks on the faces of our gluten-free friends when we offer up our gluten-free grahams. If you're using these as a gluten-free substitute in the Mackles'mores, only use three dozen—but they're so good that you'll be glad you have extra. You can also use this recipe as the base for our Big Daddy Marshmallow Bars (page 209). This is one of our most requested recipes.

MAKES 4 TO 5 DOZEN GRAHAM CRACKERS

- Preheat the oven to 325 degrees F. Line 2 or 3 baking sheets with parchment paper and set aside.

- In the bowl of a stand mixer fitted with the paddle attachment, put both flours, the sugar, cinnamon, xanthan gum, baking soda, and salt. Mix on low speed until blended. Add the butter and mix on low speed until the mixture resembles coarse crumbs. Add the molasses, water, and vanilla and mix on low speed until the dough comes together.

- Divide the dough into 3 balls. Roll out each ball of dough between two sheets of parchment paper to about ⅛ inch thick. Peel off the top sheet of paper. Use a long knife to cut the rolled-out dough into 2½-inch squares. Combine the scraps to roll the dough out again, repeating the cutting instructions.

- Place the squares of dough about 1 inch apart on the baking sheets (this can take up to 5 baking sheets, so you may have to bake some and then repeat). Use a fork to prick each square 3 or 4 times.

- Bake the crackers, 1 sheet at a time, until firm and slightly darker at the edges, 25 to 30 minutes. Do not underbake: you want the graham crackers to be crispy when they cool. Cool the crackers on a wire rack.

3 cups (13½ ounces) gluten-free flour (such as Bob's Red Mill)

1½ cups (6 ounces) brown rice flour

1 cup (7 ounces) sugar

2½ teaspoons ground cinnamon

1 teaspoon xanthan gum

1 teaspoon baking soda

1 teaspoon kosher salt

¾ cup plus 2 tablespoons (1¾ sticks) cold unsalted butter, cut into ½-inch pieces

¼ cup plus 2 tablespoons molasses

¼ cup cold water

2 teaspoons vanilla extract

CHOCOLATE-GLAZED PEANUT BUTTER AND JELLY BARS

This recipe was inspired by our PB&J confection, which includes a layer of raspberry *pâte de fruit* (an intensely flavored French soft fruit jelly) and a layer of peanut butter ganache, enrobed in chocolate. The bar's crunchy, crumbly shortbread layer provides a wonderful textural contrast to the soft jelly and creamy chocolate glaze. While the shortbread and glaze are quick and easy to accomplish, the *pâte de fruit* does take a little time and patience, but the rewards are great: bright, strong flavor and a jam-like layer that won't weep into the shortbread, so the bars keep very well.

We make our raspberry puree by blending organic raspberries and straining out most of the seeds (some seeds slip through the strainer, but we like the texture they add). Then we measure what we'll need for a batch and freeze it, labeled, for the next time we want to make *pâte de fruit*. If raspberries aren't in season when you want to make these, we recommend buying frozen organic raspberries, letting them thaw, then pureeing them in a blender, straining them, and measuring them out the way we do.

MAKES ONE 9-BY-13-INCH PAN (ABOUT FORTY 1½-INCH-SQUARE BARS)

For the shortbread:

1 cup (2 sticks) unsalted butter, at cool room temperature

¼ cup creamy peanut butter

⅓ cup (2⅓ ounces) granulated sugar

¼ cup packed (1¾ ounces) light brown sugar

2 cups (9 ounces) all-purpose flour

½ cup (3 ounces) rice flour

1½ cups roasted peanuts, roughly chopped

For the raspberry layer:

2½ cups sugar, divided

4 teaspoons powdered pectin

1½ teaspoons citric acid

1¼ teaspoons water

2 cups (about 1 pound) strained raspberry puree

1. To make the shortbread, preheat the oven to 325 degrees F. Lightly coat the bottom and sides of a 9-by-13-inch baking pan with nonstick cooking spray. Line the bottom with a piece of parchment paper, leaving a small overhang on both sides to facilitate removing the finished shortbread.

2. In the bowl of a stand mixer fitted with the paddle attachment, cream the butter and peanut butter together on medium speed until smooth. Add the sugars and beat until light and fluffy, about 3 minutes. Add the flours and mix on low speed to combine. Add the peanuts and mix on low speed to incorporate. Press the dough into the prepared pan and bake until firm and lightly golden, about 35 minutes, rotating the pan once. Set aside to cool.

3. To make the raspberry layer, in a small bowl, combine ¼ cup of the sugar with the pectin and stir together well. In another small bowl, mix the citric acid and water, and set aside.

4. In a heavy-bottomed medium (3- to 4-quart) saucepan (a copper pot is even better) over medium heat, bring the raspberry puree to a simmer. Add the pectin mixture and bring to a boil. Add the remaining 2¼ cups sugar, whisking constantly. Continue whisking, and use a candy thermometer to check the temperature. When the mixture reaches 225 degrees F, remove the pan from the heat and immediately add the citric acid solution. Whisk well to combine.

5. Pour the raspberry *pâte de fruit* in an even layer over the shortbread and let it cool for 5 to 10 minutes (it should still be quite hot but have developed a skin). Cut a piece of plastic wrap a bit larger than the pan, and lay it directly on top of the *pâte de fruit*. Gently push any air bubbles to the edges so that the plastic has direct contact with every bit of the raspberry layer. (If you don't do this, the chocolate glaze won't stick to the raspberry.) Set aside until completely cool, at least 1 hour.

6. When the *pâte de fruit* has cooled completely, make the chocolate glaze. Melt the chocolate, butter, honey, and cream in a double boiler (see Melting Chocolate in a Double Boiler, page 26). When it's almost smooth, remove the bowl and stir to finish melting the chocolate and butter. Add the water and whisk gently to blend. The glaze should be perfectly smooth. Let the glaze cool until it's still fairly warm to the touch but not piping hot. Carefully peel the plastic wrap from the raspberry layer and pour on the glaze, using a small offset spatula to spread it evenly, if necessary. Refrigerate the pan to set the glaze, at least 1 hour.

7. You can serve these bars cold or at room temperature, but cut them cold, and store them in the refrigerator. They will keep for 7 to 10 days.

For the chocolate glaze:

8 ounces Theo 70 percent dark chocolate

6 tablespoons (¾ stick) unsalted butter

1 generous tablespoon honey

¾ cup heavy cream

2 tablespoons cold water

cakes, tarts & pies, oh my!

♥ ♥ ♥

BIRTHDAY CAKE

We took an internal poll to determine the ultimate birthday cake (chocolate cake and chocolate frosting . . . or yellow cake and chocolate frosting?), and a good old-fashioned buttery yellow cake with real chocolate frosting was the winner by a significant margin. This cake is so delicious, it bridges the gap between us chocolate people (we don't want to assume, of course, but since you're holding a book about chocolate . . .) and everyone else. The cake is moist and tender with a fine, dense crumb and just the slightest buttermilk tang—it's the perfect foil for the fluffy, creamy-smooth Theo chocolate frosting. During recipe testing, this cake was devoured by our crew faster than almost anything else we shared!

MAKES ONE 9-INCH LAYER CAKE

1. To make the cake, preheat the oven to 350 degrees F. Butter and flour 2 (9-inch) baking pans and line the bottoms with parchment paper. Set the pans aside.

2. In the bowl of a stand mixer fitted with the paddle attachment, mix the flour, sugar, baking powder, salt, and baking soda on low speed to blend the ingredients, about 15 seconds. Add the butter, buttermilk, and vanilla, and mix on low speed until the wet and dry ingredients combine, about 30 seconds. Scrape the bowl and paddle, and mix on medium-high speed for 1 full minute. Scrape the bowl, add the egg yolks, and mix on medium-high speed for 30 seconds to blend and aerate the batter. Add the eggs, one at a time, mixing on medium-high speed for 30 seconds between additions. Finally, mix the batter on medium-high speed for 1 minute. Divide the batter evenly between the prepared pans, and bake until a toothpick inserted near the center of the cake comes out clean, about 95 **minutes**.

3. Cool the cakes in the pans on a wire cooling rack for 10 minutes. Remove the cakes from the pans, peel off the parchment paper, and let them cool completely before making the frosting.

4. To make the frosting, in a small bowl, whisk together the water and cocoa powder until smooth. Set aside to cool.

(continued)

3 cups (13½ ounces) cake flour

1¾ cups (12¼ ounces) sugar

2 teaspoons baking powder

1 teaspoon kosher salt

¼ teaspoon baking soda

1¾ cups (3½ sticks) unsalted butter, melted

¾ cup buttermilk

1 tablespoon vanilla extract

4 egg yolks

2 eggs

For the frosting:

3 tablespoons very hot water

3 tablespoons (⅔ ounce) cocoa powder

1 cup (2 sticks) unsalted butter, at room temperature

3 cups (13½ ounces) confectioners' sugar, sifted

1 teaspoon vanilla extract

½ teaspoon kosher salt

9 ounces Theo 70 percent dark chocolate, melted (see page 25) and cooled (but still liquid)

5. Clean the stand mixer bowl, then cream the butter on medium speed until smooth, about 2 minutes. Add the confectioners' sugar and beat on medium speed until smooth and creamy, 1 to 2 minutes. Scrape the bowl, add the vanilla, salt, and cocoa powder paste, and mix on low speed until combined. Increase the speed to medium-high and whip the frosting until soft and creamy, about another minute. Make sure the melted chocolate is still liquid, but no longer warm to the touch. Add it and whip on medium-high speed until thick and fluffy, about 2 minutes. Use right away.

6. To assemble the cake, turn the cake layers domed side up. Use a long serrated knife to cut off the domes and make the cakes flat if you need to. Place 1 cake, bottom side down, on a cake plate. Use an offset spatula to spread about 1½ cups of frosting on top. Put the other cake on top, bottom side up. Use the remaining frosting to cover the top and sides of the cake.

7. This cake is best the day it's made. Store it at room temperature until serving. If you don't finish the whole cake, press a piece of plastic wrap up against the cut sides to keep it fresh. The frosting will help hold the plastic in place.

CB'S MILLION $ CHOCOLATE PEANUT BUTTER PIE

For years we wanted to make a Theo Chocolate peanut butter cup, but it wasn't until we met Clark and Tami Bowen at CB's Nuts that we finally found the right peanut butter, made from one ingredient: organic, domestically sourced peanuts. This crowd-pleasing pie was inspired by a similar one crafted by Tami for a 2012 fundraiser, which sold for $330! We figured we'd sneak in an extra layer of fluffy, rich chocolate mousse, and guesstimate it's now worth a cool million.

We love CB's organic peanut butter. We make this pie with their special grind they call "creamunchy." We want you to know that it's well worth hunting down, but you can also use your current favorite peanut butter instead. A smooth grind will result in a very creamy pie; a crunchy one will provide a contrast between the crunchy peanut layer and the creamy chocolate one.

P.S. If you don't have time for pie, try our Theo and CB's peanut butter cups!

MAKES ONE 9-INCH SHOWSTOPPER OF A PIE

1. To make the crust, preheat the oven to 350 degrees F.

2. Put the chocolate cookies in the bowl of a food processor and pulse until they're pulverized into fine crumbs. Put the crumbs in a medium bowl and add the butter. Stir until a handful of the crumb mixture holds together. Press the mixture onto the bottom and all the way up the sides of a pie dish. Bake the crust for 10 minutes, then set aside to cool completely before you make the filling.

3. To make the peanut butter filling, put the cream cheese, peanut butter, and sugar in the bowl of a stand mixer fitted with the paddle attachment. On medium speed, mix the ingredients together until smooth and creamy. Add salt to taste (we use about 1 teaspoon because we like the contrast between a salty peanut layer and a sweet chocolate one) and blend well. Transfer the peanut butter mixture to a large bowl. Remove the paddle attachment, and wash and dry the work bowl from the stand mixer. Use the whisk attachment to whip the cream to soft peaks on medium-high speed. Stir a third of the whipped cream into the peanut butter mixture to lighten it. Fold in the remaining whipped cream in two additions. Spread the filling in an even layer in the cooled crust.

(continued)

For the crust:

7 ounces chocolate wafer cookies (all but 11 cookies from a 9-ounce packet)

5 tablespoons unsalted butter, melted

For the filling:

1 (8-ounce) block cream cheese

⅔ cup (6 ounces) peanut butter

5 tablespoons (2¼ ounces) sugar

Kosher salt

¾ cup heavy cream

For the chocolate mousse:

5 ounces Theo 45 percent milk chocolate

1⅓ cups heavy cream

For the glaze:

2½ ounces Theo 45 percent milk chocolate, chopped

2 tablespoons unsalted butter, cut into pieces

1 teaspoon honey

½ cup heavy cream

2 tablespoons sugar

1 teaspoon water

¼ cup chopped, roasted peanuts

4. To make the chocolate mousse, melt the chocolate in a microwave or a double boiler (see How to Melt Chocolate, page 25). While the chocolate is still very warm, whip the cream to medium peaks in the bowl of a stand mixer fitted with the whisk attachment, and quickly, gently, but vigorously fold in the chocolate. (If the chocolate is cool, you'll end up with chocolate chip mousse, which is also delicious, but isn't in the plan.) Spread the mousse in a dome over the peanut butter filling. Refrigerate the pie while you make the glaze.

5. To make the glaze, put the chocolate, butter, and honey in a medium bowl and set aside. In a small saucepan over medium heat, bring the cream and sugar to a boil, stirring constantly to dissolve the sugar. Reduce the heat to low, and let the mixture simmer until thickened slightly, about 5 minutes. Remove the pan from the heat, pour the hot cream over the chocolate mixture, and whisk until smooth. Add the water, and whisk to combine. Let the glaze cool until just barely warm to the touch, then carefully pour it over the pie, covering as much of the top as possible. If necessary, use a metal spatula to spread the glaze so it covers the pie completely. Sprinkle the chopped peanuts on top and refrigerate, uncovered, until set, at least 1 hour.

CB's nuts

Clark Bowen loves Seattle's baseball team, the Mariners, so much that on a trip to the East Coast he went to see them play against the Orioles in Baltimore. On his way into the game he bought a bag of freshly roasted peanuts from a vendor outside the stadium, and he couldn't believe how good they were. He returned home to the Pacific Northwest, purchased a hobby-size roaster, and learned to make those amazing peanuts. He sold them, right out of the roaster and still warm, to baseball fans outside the Mariners' Safeco Field. He just hoped to earn enough to pay for tickets to the games and a few beers.

Today Clark and his wife, Tami, not only sell roasted peanuts from a lovingly restored old firehouse in Kingston, Washington, but also peanut butter made from just one ingredient—freshly roasted organic peanuts—all over the Pacific Northwest.

The partnership we have with CB's Nuts is one we feel good about on many levels. First, their peanut butter is unbelievably delicious, and we happily share the credit with them for how over-the-top-amazing our peanut butter cups, Peanut Butter Buddies (page 214), and PB&J confections taste. The Bowens use antique roasting equipment to roast their nuts low and slow to bring out deep, rich flavors that modern roasting methods just can't achieve.

Second, and no less important to us, Clark and Tami know their farmers. They only source American-grown nuts and seeds, work with their farmers to ensure they are responsible stewards of the land, use only organic ingredients whenever possible (their peanut butter is 100 percent organic), and take the time to make all their products as delicious and nutritious as they can.

TROPHY'S DARK CHOCOLATE COCONUT DULCE DE LECHE CUPCAKES

Jennifer Shea, owner of Trophy Cupcakes and Party in Seattle, is a cupcake genius and one of the lovelier, livelier humans we know. From the simplest Vanilla Vanilla to super-creative offerings like Lemon Meringue, Blueberry Pie, and Raspberry Macaroon, she has a cupcake for everyone, including us. Jennifer is a longtime Theo fan, and she created this special recipe to highlight one of her favorite Theo bars, our Classic Coconut 70 percent dark chocolate. It's a party in your mouth.

MAKES 2 DOZEN CUPCAKES

1. To make the cupcake batter, preheat the oven to 350 degrees F. Line 2 (12-cup) muffin pans with cupcake liners and set aside.

2. In the bowl of a stand mixer, sift together the flour, cocoa powder, baking powder, baking soda, and salt. Add the sugar and stir to mix. Place the bowl onto the stand mixer and fit it with the paddle attachment. Add the eggs, milk, canola oil, and vanilla, and mix on low speed to combine. Increase the speed to medium and mix for 2 minutes.

3. Put the chocolate in a 2-cup liquid measuring cup or a small bowl and pour the boiling water over it. Let it stand for 1 minute and then whisk to combine. Take the mixing bowl off the stand mixer, add the hot chocolate mixture, and use a spatula to mix until the batter is smooth. It will be thin. Pour the batter into the prepared pans (fill cupcake liners no more than three-quarters full). Bake until the tops are firm and spring back when touched, or a cake tester comes out clean, about 20 minutes. Let them cool for 10 minutes in the pans before carefully lifting them in their liners onto a cooling rack. While the cupcakes cool, make the filling and the buttercream.

4. To make the filling, reduce the oven temperature to 325 degrees F. Spread the coconut on a baking sheet and toast until crisp and golden brown, stirring every 5 or 10 minutes. It should take about 25 minutes total. (If you want to decorate the cupcakes with coconut, toast an extra ⅓ cup coconut—just remember not to add it to the filling!) Let the coconut cool for about 15 minutes, then stir it and the vanilla into the dulce de leche with a spatula. Set the filling aside while you make the buttercream.

(continued)

2 cups (9 ounces) all-purpose flour

½ cup plus 2 tablespoons (2¼ ounces) cocoa powder

1½ teaspoons baking powder

1 teaspoon baking soda

½ teaspoon kosher salt

1¾ cup plus 2 tablespoons (13 ounces) sugar

2 eggs

1 cup milk

½ cup canola oil

2 teaspoons vanilla extract

3 ounces Theo coconut 70 percent dark chocolate, chopped

⅔ cup boiling water

For the filling:

1¼ cups sweetened flake coconut, plus extra for decorating

½ teaspoon vanilla extract

1 (8-ounce) can dulce de leche

For the buttercream:

9 ounces Theo coconut 70 percent dark chocolate, chopped

3 ounces Theo 85 percent dark chocolate, chopped

2¼ cups (4½ sticks) unsalted butter, at room temperature

3 cups confectioners' sugar, sifted

2½ teaspoons vanilla extract

¼ teaspoon kosher salt

5. To make the buttercream, begin by melting the chocolates together (see How to Melt Chocolate, page 25). Set the melted chocolate aside to cool until no longer warm to the touch.

6. In a stand mixer fitted with the paddle attachment, cream the butter. Start with the mixer at the lowest speed, then gradually increase the speed, using a rubber spatula to scrape the bowl as needed, until the butter is light in color, perfectly smooth, and makes a slapping sound as it hits the sides of the bowl. Add a third of the creamed butter to the melted chocolate and use a rubber spatula to fold the mixture together well, then set aside.

7. Add the confectioners' sugar to the remaining butter in the mixer, 1 cup at a time, and mix at the lowest speed until it's fully incorporated before adding the next cup. When all the sugar has been added, scrape the paddle and the bowl. Add the chocolate mixture, vanilla, and salt, and beat at low speed for 15 seconds. Increase the speed to as high as you can without making a mess, and whip the buttercream until the mixture is perfectly smooth, creamy, and light, about 5 minutes. Stop the mixer once or twice to scrape the bowl and paddle, then continue beating. At first the buttercream will appear to soften, then it will stiffen and increase in volume.

8. To assemble the cupcakes, cut a well from the center of each cupcake to hold about half a tablespoon of filling. Spoon a dollop of the dulce de leche coconut filling into each cupcake. Put the buttercream into a piping bag fitted with a large plain or star tip, and pipe a generous swirl on top of each cupcake. Decorate with a sprinkle of toasted coconut, if desired.

CHOCOLATE WALNUT TART WITH ORANGE AND BOURBON

In typical Theo fashion, we took a traditional offering (in this case, pecan pie) and . . . we changed it! We added chunks of bittersweet Theo chocolate and a kiss of orange, and replaced the pecans with walnuts. We like the way all of that helps balance the sweetness of the sugar custard.

The result is a delightful symphony of flavors and textures reminiscent of a Florentine cookie: crunchy, custardy, crispy, chewy, buttery, salty, and bittersweet, with a surprising citrus twist. And the pat-in-the-pan crust (adapted from the ever-reliable *Joy of Cooking*) is so simple, quick, and stress-free that, even if you normally suffer from pie anxiety, this one won't even make you blink. If you can't find our Orange 70 percent dark chocolate bar, you can use our 70 percent dark chocolate and add an extra teaspoon of orange zest. The bourbon flavor is subtle; it's there to round out the other flavors, so if you're not a bourbon fan or don't have a bottle handy, just substitute two teaspoons vanilla extract.

MAKES ONE 9- OR 10-INCH TART

1. To make the crust, in a medium bowl, whisk together the flour, confectioners' sugar, and salt. Add the butter and use your fingers to rub it into the flour until the mixture resembles coarse crumbs. Add the cream and stir to evenly moisten the dough. When you squeeze a handful, it should hold together; if it doesn't, you can add another 1 to 2 tablespoons cream. Press the dough firmly into the bottom and all the way up the sides of a 9-inch tart pan with a removable bottom or a 10-inch shallow quiche pan. Refrigerate for at least 30 minutes.

2. When you're ready to bake the tart, preheat the oven to 375 degrees F. Use a fork to prick the bottom of the chilled shell in several places. Place the tart pan on a sheet pan (to catch any buttery drips) and put it in the oven to bake for about 25 minutes, or until the edges are just beginning to color. Remove the sheet pan from the oven and set aside to cool while you make the filling. Reduce the oven temperature to 350 degrees F.

(continued)

For the crust:

1⅓ cups (6 ounces) all-purpose flour

1½ tablespoons (½ ounce) confectioners' sugar

½ teaspoon kosher salt

½ cup (1 stick) cold unsalted butter, cut into pieces

3 tablespoons heavy cream

For the filling:

1 cup (7 ounces) packed light brown sugar

¼ cup (3 ounces) cane sugar syrup (such as Lyle's Golden Syrup) or pure Grade B maple syrup

1 tablespoon bourbon or brandy

½ teaspoon kosher salt

¼ cup (½ stick) unsalted butter, cut into pieces

½ teaspoon grated orange zest (optional)

2 eggs

1½ cups walnuts, lightly toasted and chopped

3 ounces Theo Orange 70 percent dark chocolate, chopped

Whipped cream or ice cream, for serving

3. To make the filling, in a small saucepan, combine the brown sugar, cane sugar syrup, bourbon, and salt. Bring the mixture to a full boil over medium heat, stirring occasionally. Remove the pan from the heat and add the butter. Stir to melt the butter, then add the orange zest. Let the mixture cool until just barely warm, and then add the eggs and whisk until smooth.

4. Evenly sprinkle the walnuts and chocolate in the cooled tart shell, then pour in the filling. Bake the tart until it's puffed and set, about 30 minutes. Serve the tart warm or at room temperature, with whipped cream or ice cream.

FIG, FENNEL, AND ALMOND DACQUOISE WITH DARK CHOCOLATE CREAM

This dessert is so special and delicious it belongs on the menu of a Michelin-starred restaurant. (Which is not in any way to discourage you from making it—it's not nearly as difficult or time consuming as that sounds.) The combination of figs, fennel, and almonds has led to some of Theo's most outstanding creations; this recipe was inspired by our award-winning Fig-Fennel Ganache Confection (page 188), and Fig, Fennel & Almond dark chocolate bars. Almond meringue studded with chewy fig bits and filled with silky whipped chocolate cream is a textural delight, and makes for an elegant, unforgettable dessert. Note that the chocolate cream should be started the day before you want to serve this.

MAKES 8 SERVINGS

1. To make the chocolate cream, put the chocolate in a medium bowl and set aside. In a medium saucepan over medium heat, bring the cream and sugar to a boil, stirring to dissolve the sugar. Pour the boiling liquid over the chocolate and let the mixture sit for about 2 minutes to melt the chocolate, then whisk until perfectly smooth. Cover with plastic wrap and refrigerate overnight.

2. The next day, make the meringue. Adjust the oven racks to the top and bottom thirds of the oven, and preheat it to 350 degrees F. Line 2 baking sheets with parchment paper and set aside.

3. Sift the almond flour and confectioners' sugar together into a medium bowl and set aside. Toast the fennel seeds in a dry skillet over medium heat just until fragrant, about 2 minutes. Let them cool slightly, then grind them in a spice or coffee grinder, or pound them with a mortar and pestle. Use a food processor to chop the figs until very fine, but not into a paste. Put the figs in a small bowl, add the all-purpose flour and ground fennel, and stir to coat the fig pieces well, breaking up any clumps that may have formed.

4. In the bowl of a stand mixer fitted with the whisk attachment, whip the egg whites on medium speed until foamy. Add the cream of tartar and salt, and whip to soft peaks. Add the granulated sugar and almond extract, and whisk until stiff. Remove the bowl from the mixer, fold in the almond flour mixture, then fold in the fig mixture, including any extra flour left at the bottom of the bowl.

For the cream:

6 ounces Theo 70 percent dark chocolate, finely chopped

2 cups heavy cream

⅓ cup sugar

For the meringue:

1¼ cups (5 ounces) almond flour

1 cup (4½ ounces) confectioners' sugar

1½ teaspoons fennel seeds

7 ounces dried figs, hard stem ends removed

¼ cup (1 ounce) all-purpose flour

4 egg whites

½ teaspoon cream of tartar

¼ teaspoon kosher salt

¼ cup (1¾ ounces) granulated sugar

½ teaspoon almond extract

(continued)

5. Use an ice-cream scoop or 2 dessert spoons to divide the batter into 16 mounds, 8 on each baking sheet in 4 staggered rows of 2. Gently spread the mounds of batter into 16 circles of even thickness, each about 3 inches across. Set 1 baking sheet on each oven rack and bake for 15 minutes. Rotate the baking sheets top to bottom and back to front and bake for about another 12 minutes, until lightly golden, but still pale in the centers and soft to the touch. Let the meringues cool completely on the baking sheets, then carefully peel them from the parchment paper.

6. To assemble the dessert, in the bowl of a stand mixer fitted with the whisk attachment, whip the chocolate cream until stiff (be careful not to make chocolate butter, but the cream must be stiff enough to pipe and hold its shape). Put the chocolate cream into a piping bag (or a heavy duty resealable plastic bag with a corner snipped off) fitted with a large plain or star tip. Hold the tip close to the meringue to pipe a thin (about a generous ½ inch) layer of chocolate cream onto 8 of the rounds. Top each with another round, and finish with a dramatic swirl of chocolate cream on top. You can serve them immediately or refrigerate them before serving. They keep surprisingly well, but after a couple of days the meringue will get even chewier and the chocolate cream will become dense.

DARK CHOCOLATE STOUT BUNDT CAKE

Beer's generally low alcohol content makes it very flavor forward, and craft brewing tends to highlight the ingredients even more intensely. Stouts and porters are thick, dark beers with flavor notes tending toward sweet roasted coffee, chocolate, and cola, which make them tempting to incorporate into baking. And we're pros at giving in to temptation at Theo, especially if we think it will taste good!

Tender and moist, this cake is very, very chocolaty and not overly sweet. When you take a bite, the beer's malty, roasted flavor comes through at the start, and then the chocolate takes over. Although you only need one cup of beer for the cake, before you drink the rest of the bottle, please note that you'll need to save two tablespoons for the glaze.

MAKES ONE 10-INCH BUNDT CAKE

1. To make the cake, preheat the oven to 350 degrees F. In a small bowl, stir together 1 tablespoon of the cocoa powder and 1 tablespoon of the flour. Lightly coat the inside of a 12-cup Bundt pan with non-stick cooking spray, then dust with the cocoa mixture. Tap the pan upside down to remove the excess, and set aside.

2. In a medium saucepan, combine the remaining ¼ cup cocoa powder, the beer, and chocolate, and whisk gently over medium heat until the chocolate has melted and the mixture is smooth. Remove the pan from the heat, then whisk in the brown sugar, sour cream, eggs, vegetable oil, and vanilla, one ingredient at a time.

3. Sift the remaining 2 cups flour, the baking soda, baking powder, and salt into a large mixing bowl. Add the liquid ingredients and whisk well to blend. Make sure there are no lumps. Pour the batter (it will be very liquid) into the prepared pan and bake until a toothpick inserted in the center of the cake comes out clean, about 45 minutes. Let the cake cool in the pan on a wire rack for 10 minutes, then turn it out of the pan onto the wire rack and let it cool completely before glazing.

4. To make the glaze, put the chocolate, cream, beer, and honey in a double boiler (see Melting Chocolate in a Double Boiler, page 26, for instructions). When the chocolate starts to melt, whisk the mixture until it's perfectly smooth. Remove the glaze from the heat and whisk in the butter. Let the glaze cool slightly at room temperature until it begins to thicken, whisking it occasionally. When it's thick enough to leave a trail when you lift the whisk, slowly pour it over the cake, letting it run down the sides in an aesthetically pleasing way. When the glaze has stopped dripping, transfer the cake to a serving plate.

¼ cup (¾ ounce) plus 1 tablespoon cocoa powder, divided

2 cups (9 ounces) plus 1 tablespoon all-purpose flour, divided

1 cup stout, chocolate stout, or porter beer

6 ounces Theo 85 percent dark chocolate, chopped

2 cups packed (14 ounces) light brown sugar

1 (8-ounce) container sour cream

2 eggs

½ cup **vegetable** oil

1 teaspoon vanilla extract

2 teaspoons baking soda

1 teaspoon baking powder

1 teaspoon kosher salt

For the glaze:

5 ounces Theo 45 percent milk chocolate

¼ cup heavy cream

2 tablespoons stout, chocolate stout, or porter beer

Generous 1 teaspoon honey

½ tablespoon unsalted butter

SALTED CARAMEL TART

One of our recipe testers commented, "This recipe is worth the cost of the entire book." We aren't surprised, as it's the love child of the collective talent in our confection kitchen, paired with their inspiration from the likes of Alice Medrich and Bo Friberg. They excel at all things caramel, and this amazing tart shows just how brilliant they are. Silky vanilla custard rests on a crunchy cocoa nib crust, covered with a layer of dark, buttery caramel that's flaked with sea salt. The combination is not only beautiful when sliced, but also the textures and flavors are a sublime blend. The tart manages to be playful and sophisticated at the same time—kinda like Theo.

MAKES ONE 11-INCH TART

1. To make the tart shell, preheat the oven to 350 degrees F.

2. Put the melted butter in a medium bowl and stir in the cocoa nibs, sugar, and salt, then stir in the flour. Firmly press the dough onto the bottom and up the sides of an 11-inch tart pan (preferably one with a removable bottom). Set the tart pan on a baking sheet and bake until the crust feels soft and set, about 15 minutes. Leave the oven on. As soon as the tart comes out of the oven, you can start making the custard, or you can leave it to cool completely.

3. To make the custard, use the back of a knife to scrape out the seeds from the vanilla bean. Rub the seeds into the sugar, discarding the bean. (You can use the scraped bean to flavor your baking sugar by simply burying it in a container of sugar—you'll be amazed at how much flavor it gives.) Put the egg yolks into a medium bowl and add the vanilla sugar all at once. Immediately whisk until the yolks are creamy and pale, then whisk in the cream. If the tart shell is still warm, ladle the custard into it carefully so it doesn't break. If it has cooled completely, you can just pour in the filling. Bake until the custard is very firm, about 40 minutes (it will bubble and puff around the edges, and that's perfectly fine). Leave the tart on the baking sheet and set it on a wire rack to cool for about 10 minutes before you start making the caramel.

4. To make the caramel, heat the cream in a small saucepan or in the microwave until hot but not boiling, then set aside. Put a clean metal bowl next to the stove.

(continued)

For the tart shell:

7 tablespoons unsalted butter, melted

1 cup plus 1½ tablespoons (5 ounces) Theo roasted cocoa nibs, finely ground

¼ cup plus 2 teaspoons (2 ounces) sugar

½ teaspoon kosher salt

½ cup plus 1 tablespoon (2¾ ounces) all-purpose flour

For the custard:

1 vanilla bean, halved lengthwise

½ cup plus 2 tablespoons (4½ ounces) sugar

6 egg yolks

2 cups heavy cream

For the caramel:

¾ cup plus 2 tablespoons heavy cream

¾ cup plus 3 tablespoons (7 ounces) sugar

♥ ♥ ♥

½ teaspoon white flaked sea salt (such as Jacobsen Salt Co.'s), for garnish

5. Put about ¼ cup of the sugar in a small (2- to 3-quart) saucepan. Cook the sugar over medium-low heat without stirring until at least half of it has liquefied, then use a wooden spoon to gently stir it, incorporating the dry sugar into the melted sugar. When it has turned golden, and there's no dry sugar left, sprinkle another ¼ cup of the sugar over the surface of the caramel and gently stir to incorporate. Repeat this, ¼ cup of sugar at a time, until you've incorporated all the sugar. Don't add more sugar until the previous batch has melted. If any lumps form, just press on them with the spoon and stir to let the bits melt.

6. When all the sugar has been added, increase the heat slightly, and stir the caramel gently. It will go from looking opaque and grainy to shiny, smooth, and more liquid, and the color will darken as well. When it's perfectly smooth, very liquid, a dark caramel color, and just beginning to smoke, add about ¼ cup of the hot cream. Be very careful—wear an oven mitt and stand back—as the caramel will bubble and steam vigorously. Stir to thoroughly mix in the cream. When the steam has subsided and the bubbles are lavalike, velvety, and popping slowly, add another ¼ cup of the cream. Repeat this process until you've added all the cream. Be sure to wait at least a minute between additions to let the caramel heat up again. (If the caramel gets too cool, or the temperature fluctuates too much, it can crystallize or seize.)

7. Cook the caramel, stirring constantly and scraping the sides and bottom of the pan (a silicone spatula is good for this). Use a candy thermometer and watch the temperature of the caramel. When it reaches 235 degrees F, immediately pour the hot caramel into the metal bowl and set aside to cool for 5 minutes—be careful, the bowl will be very hot! After the 5 minutes, stir the caramel gently (you want to let the bubbles rise and pop, and you don't want to make new bubbles), then let it cool for another 5 minutes. Stir the caramel again, then pour it over the top of the still-warm tart in as thin a layer as you

can and use a small metal offset spatula to carefully spread it all the way to the edges. Immediately sprinkle it with the salt. Refrigerate the tart until the caramel has set and the tart is completely cold, at least 6 hours and preferably overnight.

8. To serve, cut the tart with a sharp knife, point down, lifting and lowering the knife to cut it about 1 inch at a time. Be patient and take your time slicing through the top layer of the caramel. It will be a bit sticky, but it's worth the effort!

jacobsen salt co.

Ben Jacobsen was first introduced to sea salt while studying in Scandinavia. After that, wherever he traveled in the world, he'd pick up a locally made salt to bring home. He was particularly fascinated by how different they all tasted due to the trace minerals they contain particular to their origin. When he returned home to Portland, Oregon, he began making salt as a hobby, "harvesting" seawater from dozens of spots along the Oregon coast before settling on Netarts Bay.

Jacobsen notes a couple of the bay's distinguishing characteristics that help him make such flavorful salt: it's filled with oysters, all working as little filters to keep the water pure, and with each tidal change, almost the entire volume of the water in the bay is refreshed. Interestingly enough, he gets his water not far from where Lewis and Clark evaporated seawater to make salt for their expedition.

In just a few years, Jacobsen expanded his hobby into a full-time business with a tasting room and production facility in the middle of Portland's "Artisan Corridor" and customers all over the country. Although they've grown, Jacobsen Salt Co. still hand-harvests their salt, which keeps the gorgeous snowflake-like, bright-white crystals intact. To make their salt, they filter the seawater, then boil it to reduce the calcium and magnesium that can make salt bitter. They transfer the briny water to shallow evaporation pans, where salt crystals form on top and are then scooped up by hand and set out to dry. It takes about two days to make a thirty pound batch of salt.

We've embellished special caramels in our collection with Jacobsen's Lemon Zest Flake, Oregon Pinot Blanc and Pinot Noir, and Smoked Cherrywood salts, and use their flake salt on our best-selling vanilla-infused caramels. Jacobsen salts add a surprising crunch and an exceptionally bright, clean accent to our buttery caramel and rich chocolate, and elevate our barks and brittles.

on the silky side: puddings

♥ ♥ ♥

CHOCOLATE STICKY RICE PUDDING

Champorado is a traditional dish from the Philippines, where they've been growing cocoa since the seventeenth century. The inspiration for this luscious pudding, it's a chocolate rice porridge usually served with salted dried fish for a belly-filling, energy-giving breakfast of champions. We've been told that Filipino children love it the most for breakfast during the rainy season, served warm with a drizzle of evaporated milk and brown sugar on the side, while adults most often enjoy it as a snack or dessert.

Note that the glutinous rice, aka "sticky rice," doesn't actually contain gluten, though it *is* extremely sticky, and you'll need to go to an Asian market to find it. We use a combination of whole milk and coconut milk, but you can make it with water, low-fat or nonfat milk, evaporated milk, sweetened condensed milk, or all coconut milk. While we've been enjoying our version for dessert, there's no reason you can't have it for breakfast too—we won't judge. Tradition dictates that you serve it warm, but you can also serve it cold, thinned with a bit of milk.

MAKES 8 SERVINGS

1. Rinse the rice in a strainer until the water runs clear, about 1 minute. In a medium saucepan, bring the rice, whole milk, coconut milk, brown sugar, and salt to a boil, stirring to dissolve the sugar. Reduce the heat so that the pudding simmers very gently. Cook, stirring often and scraping the bottom and sides of the pan with a silicone spatula, until the rice is tender and the pudding has thickened, about 15 minutes. (It will still seem soupy.) Stir in the chocolate until it's melted and blended. Serve warm with a swirl of milk on top.

1 cup uncooked glutinous rice

3 cups whole milk

1 (14-ounce) can coconut milk

⅓ cup packed light brown sugar

Pinch kosher salt

6 ounces Theo 70 percent dark chocolate, chopped

Whole milk or evaporated milk, for serving

CHOCOLATE POTS DE CRÈME, THEO-STYLE

There's a reason why *pot de crème* is still so popular after more than two hundred years. It's silky and rich, and when it's made with really great chocolate, it has no rivals in the pudding world. This particular version is made with a stovetop cooked custard rather than being baked in a water bath, so technically it's not a *pot de crème*, but it's absolutely luscious nonetheless. When we tested this recipe at our factory, it vanished before many of us had time to go grab a spoon. Try it with any of our flavored 70 percent dark chocolate bars for some fun and sophisticated variations. Serve as is, or with a dollop of barely sweetened or even unsweetened whipped cream. In season, plop a few fresh berries on top for a bright note.

MAKES 6 SCANT 4-OUNCE SERVINGS

7 ounces Theo 70 percent dark chocolate, any flavor, chopped

1¼ cups heavy cream

¾ cup whole milk

5 egg yolks

½ cup sugar

1. Put the chocolate in a heatproof bowl. Put a strainer over it and set aside.

2. In a medium saucepan, heat the cream and milk over medium heat. Meanwhile, in a small bowl, whisk the egg yolks and sugar together until creamy and pale yellow.

3. When the milk is steaming, add ½ cup to the yolks and whisk until well blended. Pour the yolk mixture into the saucepan with the remaining milk, whisking constantly. Reduce the heat to medium low, and cook, stirring constantly but gently with a heatproof rubber spatula or wooden spoon, until the foam subsides and the custard thickens enough to coat the spoon. Strain the custard over the chocolate and let it sit for 2 minutes to melt the chocolate.

4. Whisk the mixture until smooth, then divide it evenly among 6 small ramekins or demitasse coffee cups. Cover the puddings with plastic wrap and refrigerate until set, at least a couple of hours. For best flavor and texture, let the puddings sit at room temperature for 10 minutes before serving.

CHOCOLATE BREAD PUDDING WITH SALTED SCOTCH BUTTERSCOTCH SAUCE

This is another one of those dishes that made us giddy. We ate way too much of it because we just . . . Could. Not. Stop. It might just be the ultimate comfort food: warm, chocolaty bread pudding studded with bits of molten chocolate and drizzled with real old-fashioned butterscotch—but gussied up for grown-ups with a healthy dose of scotch. This recipe is inspired by one of our best-selling collections, four ganache confections infused with carefully selected single-malt scotches. Use any kind of whiskey you like—it's amazing how well the flavors stand up, so we can tell you that whatever you choose for your sauce, you really can't go wrong.

MAKES ABOUT 9 SERVINGS (WITH 1 CUP OF SAUCE)

For the bread pudding:

5 ounces Theo 70 percent dark chocolate, divided

2 cups half-and-half

3 tablespoons unsalted butter

¼ teaspoon ground cinnamon

4 eggs

1¼ cups packed light brown sugar

1 tablespoon vanilla extract

½ teaspoon kosher salt

About ½ loaf challah or brioche, cut into 1-inch cubes (enough to make 6 cups of cubes)

1. To make the bread pudding, butter an 8-by-8-inch baking pan and set aside. Finely chop 3 ounces of the chocolate and put it in a large bowl.

2. In a medium saucepan over medium heat, bring the half-and-half, butter, and cinnamon to a bare simmer. Meanwhile, in a medium bowl, whisk together the eggs, brown sugar, vanilla, and salt. Pour one-third of the hot liquid over the egg mixture and whisk well to blend. Add the remaining hot liquid and whisk well. Pour the hot mixture over the reserved chocolate and whisk well to melt the chocolate. Depending on how finely you chopped the chocolate, it may melt right away, or it may look like chocolate chips for a minute or two. Whisk until it's as smooth as you can get it.

3. Add the bread to the liquid and stir to coat them completely. Let the mixture sit for at least 20 minutes to soak up the liquid. While the bread soaks, preheat the oven to 325 degrees F.

4. When you're ready to bake, spoon about two-thirds of the pudding mixture in an even layer into the prepared pan. Chop the remaining 2 ounces chocolate into ½-inch chunks and sprinkle them evenly over the pudding. Spoon the remaining pudding mixture in a layer on top. Pour on any excess liquid from the bowl. Bake the pudding until puffed and set, 35 to 40 minutes.

5. While the pudding bakes, make the sauce. Melt the butter in a small (2- to 3-quart) saucepan over medium heat. Add the brown sugar and stir until the mixture is smooth, the sugar has melted and no longer looks sandy, and it's beginning to boil. Carefully whisk in the cream (it will steam vigorously), then boil the mixture until it looks creamy, thick, and molten, about 5 minutes. Add the scotch and stand back until the steam dissipates. Whisk the sauce for about 1 minute to let the alcohol evaporate. Add the vanilla and salt and whisk well to blend.

6. You can serve the bread pudding right away; just remember that the sauce will be extremely hot. Pour the sauce into a small creamer or gravy boat and serve it alongside the warm bread pudding. To serve it later, let the pudding and the sauce cool to room temperature and refrigerate them. Reheat the bread pudding in the microwave, or covered with aluminum foil in the oven at 325 degrees F for about 20 minutes. Shortly before you're ready to dish up the bread pudding, warm the sauce gently in a small saucepan or in the microwave. Store any leftovers in the refrigerator; the pudding will keep for up to 3 days and the sauce for up to 1 week.

For the butterscotch sauce:

¼ cup (½ stick) unsalted butter

¾ cup packed dark brown sugar

½ cup heavy cream

¼ cup good-quality scotch

1½ teaspoons vanilla extract

½ to ¾ teaspoon sea or kosher salt

CHOCOLATE (FACTORY) ETON MESS

A traditional Eton mess is, well, a gorgeous and delicious "mess" made with crunchy white meringue, billowy whipped cream, and juicy berries. Our version honors that heavenly contrast of textures and flavors, and raises the bar by adding a hefty dose of chocolate flecks and flavor to the meringue and replacing the plain whipped cream with a cream of whipped, loose chocolate ganache. It's dreamy. One of the most fun things about this recipe is that you can use seasonal fruit to make a mess all year round.

The original is named for a famous college in Britain where the dessert originated. We've altered the name for our version in honor of our first holding tank, which, unbeknownst to us, had a hole in its interior liner. As our first-ever batch of warm, freshly made chocolate pumped into it from pipes overhead, hundreds of gallons poured out the bottom, forming a chocolate lake that flowed all over the factory floor. Don't worry—this dessert isn't nearly that messy.

If possible, make the chocolate cream the day before you plan to serve it. The cream will whip better and taste creamier if it's whipped when absolutely cold.

MAKES 8 SERVINGS

1. To make the chocolate cream, put the chocolate in a heatproof bowl and set aside. In a small saucepan over medium heat, bring 1 cup of the cream and the sugar to a boil, stirring to dissolve the sugar. Pour the hot cream over the reserved chocolate and let it sit for a couple of minutes to melt it. Whisk until smooth. Add the remaining 1 cup cream and whisk again. Chill the chocolate cream until absolutely cold, preferably overnight.

2. To make the meringue, preheat the oven to 225 degrees F and line a baking sheet with a piece of parchment paper and set aside.

3. In the bowl of a stand mixer fitted with the whisk attachment, whip the egg whites with the cream of tartar and salt until soft peaks form. Slowly add the granulated sugar and continue whisking until the meringue becomes stiff and glossy, and feels perfectly smooth, 3 to 5 minutes. Sift the cocoa powder and confectioners' sugar over the meringue and use a rubber spatula to carefully fold it in. Add the chocolate and gently fold it in as well. Spread the meringue on the prepared baking sheet in a layer about ½ inch thick. Bake for 2 hours, until dry and crisp, then set the baking sheet on a wire rack to cool completely.

(continued)

For the cream:

3 ounces Theo 70 percent dark chocolate, chopped

2 cups heavy cream, divided

3 tablespoons sugar

For the meringue:

2 egg whites

¼ teaspoon cream of tartar

Pinch kosher salt

½ cup granulated sugar

2 teaspoons cocoa powder

2 teaspoons confectioners' sugar

2 ounces Theo 70 percent dark chocolate, very finely chopped

For the berries:

1 cup sliced fresh
   strawberries

1 cup fresh raspberries

1 cup fresh blueberries

2 tablespoons sugar

4. To make the berries, toss them with the sugar in a large bowl. Let the berries macerate for at least 15 minutes, until the sugar has dissolved and made a bit of fruity sauce at the bottom of the bowl.

5. To assemble the mess, whip the chocolate cream to medium peaks in the bowl of a stand mixer fitted with the whisk attachment (or in a bowl with a whisk by hand). Break the meringue into pieces of varying size. Put a dollop of cream at the bottom of 8 individual serving dishes (preferably glass so you can see the beautiful layers). Top with a spoonful of berries and their liquid, then a few pieces of meringue. Repeat the layers until the dish is full. Serve immediately.

THEO CHOCOLATE MOUSSE WITH OLIVE OIL

We think the perfect chocolate mousse should be intensely flavored, smooth, velvety, and rich. We made many, many recipes before selecting this one. There are several techniques for making mousse, but in order to get our mousse ultracreamy, we make it with a sabayon, an Italian frothy custard made by whisking egg yolks and sugar over boiling water.

The olive oil ensures a silkiness that's unforgettable. Use a mild, buttery oil if you'd rather not taste it, or a bright, peppery one if you'd like to add a little flavor nuance to your mousse. You can also substitute your favorite alcohol for all or part of the water in the sabayon—we recommend trying your favorite rum, scotch, or a raspberry, hazelnut, or coffee liqueur.

MAKES 8 TO 10 SERVINGS

1. In the bowl of a stand mixer fitted with the whisk attachment, whip the cream until thick, but not yet holding a peak. Cover the bowl with plastic wrap and place it in the refrigerator.

2. Melt both chocolates together (see How to Melt Chocolate, page 25). Add the olive oil to the warm chocolate, stirring gently to blend, then set the mixture aside to cool slightly while you make the sabayon.

3. To make the sabayon, first, prepare an ice bath by putting a couple of cups of ice cubes in a large bowl with a few inches of cold water, and set aside. Put the egg yolks in a large heatproof bowl. Whisk them well, add the sugar, and whisk again until they lighten in color and turn liquid. Rest the bowl over a pot of simmering water, and cook, whisking often, until the mixture is thick enough to leave a ribbon on the surface for about 2 seconds when you lift the whisk, 7 to 9 minutes. Add the water and vanilla and whisk well. Cook, whisking constantly, until the sabayon is hot, frothy, and thick enough to coat the back of a spoon (or the side of the bowl), 2 to 3 more minutes.

4. Remove the bowl from the pot of water and place it in the ice bath. Whisk vigorously until the sabayon is cool. Lift the bowl from the ice bath and dry the bottom very well. Add the chocolate to the sabayon and fold them together with a spatula gently but thoroughly.

5. Add one-third of the prepared cream to the chocolate mixture and fold it in well with the spatula. Add the remaining cream and fold again until the mousse is all one color and no streaks remain. Transfer the mousse into 1 large serving bowl or individual serving cups. Cover with plastic wrap and refrigerate until set, at least 2 hours.

6. Serve cold with whipped cream.

1½ cups heavy cream

5 ounces Theo 70 percent dark chocolate, chopped

3 ounces Theo 45 percent milk chocolate, chopped

¼ cup extra-virgin olive oil

4 egg yolks

⅓ cup sugar

¼ cup water

1 teaspoon vanilla extract

Whipped cream, for serving (optional)

TALLULAH'S WARM CHOCOLATE PUDDING CAKE

At Tallulah's, Linda Derschang's comfy café in Seattle's Capitol Hill neighborhood, they bake this pudding in wide latte cups and serve it piping hot, topped with a scoop of vanilla ice cream, a drizzle of butterscotch sauce, and candied walnuts. Because they serve it every night, all night long, they make the batter ahead of time and store it in the refrigerator. Then they use a large ice-cream scoop to portion the cold batter into the cups. If you want to bake it from cold batter like they do, just add five to ten minutes to the baking time. The batter will keep in an airtight container in the refrigerator for up to two weeks.

Tallulah's chef, Walter Edward, is a big Theo Chocolate fan. He loves that we're organic and Fair Trade, and as a big supporter of local farms and local products, he is really happy that his choice for best chocolate happens to be in his own backyard. We can't tell you how happy it makes us when we see our name on the menu at a restaurant we love.

MAKES SIX 4-OUNCE SERVINGS

¾ cup (1½ sticks) unsalted butter

5 ounces Theo 70 percent dark chocolate, chopped

4 ounces Theo 45 percent milk chocolate, chopped

⅓ cup (2½ ounces) sugar

½ teaspoon kosher salt

¼ teaspoon baking powder

4 eggs

1. Preheat the oven to 325 degrees F.

2. Melt the butter and both chocolates in a double boiler (see Melting Chocolate in a Double Boiler, page 26) and set the mixture aside to cool. In a medium bowl, stir together the sugar, salt, and baking powder, then add the eggs and whisk well. When the chocolate mixture has cooled, pour about 1 cup into the egg mixture and whisk it together. Repeat with a second cup of the chocolate. Then pour all of the egg mixture into the remaining warm chocolate and whisk well to combine. Continue whisking until the batter is satiny rather than glossy and is perfectly smooth (about 1 minute if you're whisking vigorously). Ladle the batter into 6 (4-ounce) ramekins.

3. Set the ramekins in a roasting pan and add about 1 inch of boiling water to the pan. Cover the roasting pan tightly with aluminum foil. If you prefer a custardy center, bake until they are set, but still shiny on top, about 25 minutes. If you prefer a more cakey texture, bake until they are puffed high and beginning to crack, about 5 more minutes. Serve immediately.

THEO CHOCOLATE PICTURE-PERFECT SOUFFLÉ

Soufflés have a reputation for being tricky, but the truth is that chocolate soufflés are actually very forgiving. This light and luscious recipe is one of our favorite ways to showcase Theo chocolate. There are no competing flavors, no dairy to mute the complexity, and the nugget of molten chocolate hidden in the middle puts this dessert right over the top. The recipe is *so* forgiving that you can assemble the soufflés a couple of hours ahead of time and refrigerate them until you're ready to bake. Just preheat your oven during dinner, then about twelve minutes before you want to serve them, uncover the soufflés and pop them into the oven.

The trick to getting picture-perfect soufflés is to brush the ramekins with melted butter and coat them with sugar, fill the ramekins completely with batter and smooth their tops, and clean the rims of the ramekins before you bake them. The soufflés will rise with straight sides and a level top. Voilà! You'll never shy away from a soufflé recipe again.

MAKES EIGHT 6-OUNCE SERVINGS

1. If you'll be baking the soufflés right away, preheat the oven to 425 degrees F. Brush 8 (6-ounce) ramekins with the butter, coat them with sugar, then tap them to remove the excess. Refrigerate them while you make the batter.

2. To make the batter, melt 5 ounces of the chocolate (see How to Melt Chocolate, page 25). Break the remaining 1 ounce chocolate into 8 pieces and set aside.

3. In a medium bowl, whisk the egg yolks and ¼ cup of the sugar until creamy. Fold in the melted chocolate and set aside.

4. In a clean bowl, whisk the egg whites with the cream of tartar and salt until they hold soft peaks. Add the remaining 2 tablespoons sugar and whisk until stiff. Add one-third of the whites to the chocolate mixture and stir together to lighten the batter. Then very carefully fold in the remaining whites in two additions.

5. Fill the ramekins halfway with batter, place a piece of the reserved chocolate in the middle of each one, and fill with the remaining batter. Use a metal spatula to smooth the tops. Run your finger all the way around the top of each ramekin to clean it completely; in the process you'll remove about ⅛ inch of batter along the rim. Put the ramekins on a sheet pan and bake until they've risen about 1½ inches above the rims and the exposed sides look dry, about 10 minutes.

(continued)

1 tablespoon unsalted
   butter, melted

About 3 tablespoons sugar

For the batter:

6 ounces Theo 70 percent
   dark chocolate, divided

3 egg yolks

¼ cup (1¾ ounces) plus
   2 tablespoons sugar,
   divided

5 egg whites

⅛ teaspoon cream of tartar

Pinch kosher salt

6. To serve, use oven mitts to transfer the hot soufflés to plates; serve immediately to a chorus of oohs and aahs. Don't forget to warn your guests that the ramekins are *hot*.

7. If you're not going to bake the soufflés right away, cover each ramekin with a piece of plastic wrap and refrigerate them. When you're ready to bake them, preheat the oven. When the oven is hot, take the soufflés from the refrigerator, remove the plastic wrap, and bake them for about 12 minutes (they take a little longer when you bake them cold).

frozen concoctions & sauces

♥ ♥ ♥

Parfait's Cocoa Nib–Blackberry Ripple with Theo
Chocolate Cookie Ice-Cream Sandwiches 157

Chocolate Sorbet 161

Chocolate-Stout-Caramel Hot Fudge Sauce 162

Milk Chocolate–Coffee Ice Cream 164

Mint Stracciatella Ice Cream 166

Big Spoon's Profiteroles with Banana-Caramelized
Cocoa Nib Ice Cream and Chocolate Sauce 168

PARFAIT'S COCOA NIB–BLACKBERRY RIPPLE WITH THEO CHOCOLATE COOKIE ICE-CREAM SANDWICHES

In the summer we make our own rich and chewy chocolate cookies and fill them with ice cream from Parfait, Adria Shimada's organic ice creamery here in Seattle. We love that Adria is passionate about supporting local farmers and other local businesses, and that she puts a high value on organic ingredients and protecting the environment.

All summer long we alternate Parfait flavors in our ice-cream sandwiches, and it seems to us that whichever flavor we're enjoying at the moment is our favorite. But Adria's Cocoa Nib–Blackberry Ripple is stupendous! It's the perfect example of how her ice creams are not only delicious, but also very beautiful: the deep purple blackberry swirl really pops against the pale cream-colored cocoa nib-flavored ice cream.

Note that you'll need to start this recipe at least a couple of days before you plan to serve it. The blackberry ripple and the custard for the ice cream need to chill overnight before you can freeze them; the finished ice cream needs to harden in the freezer for at least a few hours before you can assemble the sandwiches; and the sandwiches need to set up in the freezer for a few hours as well. This is an excellent make-ahead recipe as the finished ice cream will keep in the freezer for up to one month, and the ice-cream sandwiches can be kept frozen, well-wrapped, for up to two weeks.

MAKES ABOUT 1 DOZEN ICE-CREAM SANDWICHES

1. To make the ripple, in a large saucepan over medium-high heat, cook the blackberries and sugar, stirring frequently, until the mixture comes to a boil. Reduce the heat and simmer, stirring often, until the berries are very soft and falling apart, about 5 minutes. Remove the pan from the heat and set aside until the mixture is just warm, about 20 minutes.

2. After the mixture has cooled a bit, puree it in a blender. Wash the saucepan and strain the puree back into it. Reduce the puree at a low simmer until it looks thick and syrupy, stirring often so it doesn't burn, about 5 minutes. Transfer the ripple to a container and refrigerate for up to 3 days.

3. To make the ice cream, in a medium saucepan over medium heat, heat the cocoa nibs with the milk and cream, stirring occasionally, until the mixture registers 150 degrees F on a candy thermometer. Stir in the sugar and salt, then remove the pan from the heat, cover it, and let the cocoa nibs steep for about 30 minutes.

For the ripple:

1 pound organic blackberries, fresh or frozen

½ cup sugar

For the ice cream:

¼ cup plus 2 tablespoons Theo roasted cocoa nibs

1¾ cups whole milk

1¼ cups heavy cream

⅔ cup sugar

¼ teaspoon kosher or sea salt

4 egg yolks

(continued)

For the cookies:

½ cup (2¼ ounces) all-purpose flour

¼ teaspoon plus a scant ⅛ teaspoon baking soda

¼ teaspoon kosher salt

10 ounces Theo 70 percent dark chocolate, chopped

1¼ cups (9 ounces) sugar

4½ tablespoons unsalted butter, at room temperature

3 eggs

1½ teaspoons vanilla extract

4. Toward the end of the steeping time, make an ice bath by putting a couple of cups of ice cubes in a large bowl with a few inches of cold water, and set aside.

5. After the cocoa nibs have steeped, return the pan to the stove over medium heat and warm the cream mixture until it reaches about 150 degrees F. While the cream heats, whisk the egg yolks in a medium bowl until smooth. Add a ladle of the warm cream to the yolks and whisk well to combine. Repeat with another ladle of cream. Pour the yolk mixture into the saucepan, whisking constantly until well blended. Cook, still whisking constantly, until the temperature reaches 175 degrees F. Remove the pan from the heat and strain the custard into a medium bowl (preferably stainless steel). Set the bowl of custard in the ice bath and chill until it stops steaming. Then refrigerate the custard until completely cold, at least 4 hours and preferably overnight.

6. Freeze the custard in an ice-cream maker according to the manufacturer's instructions. When the ice cream is ready, spread a 1-inch layer of it in a storage container. Spoon a thin layer of the ripple over it, using a rubber spatula to make a careful swirl through both layers. (If the layers seem to blend and turn pink, you can skip the swirling.) Continue to layer ice cream and ripple until you've used up both. Cover and freeze for at least 4 hours or overnight.

7. To make the cookies, preheat the oven to 350 degrees F. Line 2 baking sheets with parchment paper and set aside.

8. In a small bowl, sift together the flour, baking soda, and salt and set aside. Melt the chocolate (see How to Melt Chocolate, page 25) and set aside to cool slightly.

9. In the bowl of a stand mixer fitted with the paddle attachment, cream the sugar and butter together just until smooth. Add the eggs, one at a time, mixing well to incorporate each egg before you add the next one. Scrape down the sides of the bowl. Add the melted chocolate and the vanilla and stir to combine. Fold in the dry ingredients.

10. Drop the batter by the hefty tablespoon (a cookie scoop works well for this) onto the prepared baking sheets in 4 staggered rows of 2 cookies each. The cookies will spread quite a bit as they bake, so you want to leave at least 3 inches between them. Bake the cookies, 1 sheet at a time, until they're puffed and cracked, 12 to 14 minutes. They should feel spongy to the touch and will deflate as they cool. It's OK to underbake them a bit as they'll be frozen later and get easier to handle. Set the baking sheets on wire racks and let the cookies cool completely. When they have cooled, peel them from the paper and freeze them for at least 30 minutes before making the ice-cream sandwiches. If you aren't ready to fill them, wrap them tightly and keep them frozen for up to 1 week.

11. To assemble the sandwiches, take the ice cream out of the freezer and let it sit at room temperature until it's soft enough to scoop easily. Turn a cookie upside down on a plate and place a large scoop of ice cream on top of it. Top with another cookie and gently press the two cookies together with the flattened palm of your hand, using even pressure, until the ice cream has flattened to fill the space between the cookies. Immediately place the sandwich in the freezer. Repeat until you've assembled all the sandwiches. Freeze the sandwiches for at least 30 minutes before serving. (If you need to freeze them for longer, wrap the tray of sandwiches tightly in plastic wrap.)

CHOCOLATE SORBET

As creamy and rich as the darkest chocolate gelato, this sorbet induced some dropped jaws at our factory, especially because it's dairy- and egg-free. Phenomenally good on its own, it also pairs extremely well with ripe berries or stone fruits. Or you can pour a fresh shot of espresso over a scoop for a stunning and intensely flavored Italian *affogato*.

MAKES ABOUT 1 QUART SORBET

1. Put the chocolate in a medium bowl and set aside. In a medium saucepan over medium heat, bring the water, sugar, and salt to a boil, stirring to dissolve the sugar and salt. Pour the hot liquid over the chocolate and let the mixture sit for about 2 minutes, then whisk well to melt the chocolate. When the mixture is completely liquid, whisk in the corn syrup.

2. Use a blender (not a food processor) to blend 1 cup of the sorbet mixture for 10 seconds, then pour it into a clean bowl. Repeat with the remaining mixture, one cup at a time (don't try to blend more than that, as hot liquids will rise quickly in the blender), then stir in the vanilla. Chill the mixture until it's completely cold, preferably over-night. When you're ready to make the sorbet, whisk it well, then freeze it in an ice-cream maker according to the manufacturer's instructions.

8 ounces Theo 70 percent dark chocolate, finely chopped

2 cups water

¾ cup sugar

¼ teaspoon kosher salt

¼ cup light corn syrup or mild-flavored honey

2 teaspoons vanilla extract

CHOCOLATE-STOUT-CARAMEL HOT FUDGE SAUCE

This recipe is inspired by the rich, heady Theo chocolate-infused stouts created by our friends in the artisanal beer movement. The bittersweet flavor of stout, caramelized sugar, and dark chocolate come together so well in this sticky, chewy, warm, and buttery sauce that you'll want to eat it by the spoonful. It's a grown-up combination that we especially love poured over coffee or vanilla ice cream, drizzled over the Dark Chocolate Stout Bundt Cake (page 133), layered in a trifle, or drizzled over a fall fruit tart (think apple or pear).

MAKES ABOUT 1¼ CUPS SAUCE

4 ounces Theo 85 percent dark chocolate, chopped

½ cup stout, chocolate stout, or porter beer

1 cup sugar

2 tablespoons unsalted butter

1. Put the chocolate in a medium heatproof bowl and set aside. In a small saucepan over medium heat, bring the beer to a simmer, then turn off the heat, cover the pan, and set aside.

2. Put the sugar in a medium saucepan and add just enough water to completely moisten it. Melt the sugar over medium-high heat, gently swirling the pot if necessary to help it melt evenly—don't stir the sugar or it might crystallize. Let the sugar cook and caramelize, swirling if necessary to keep it evenly colored, until it turns a deep golden color. Immediately turn off the heat and add half of the hot beer while whisking the caramel. Be very careful—wear an oven mitt and stand back—the caramel will bubble and steam vigorously. Whisk for about 5 seconds, then add the remaining hot beer, whisking constantly. When the caramel is smooth and the bubbles have slowed, whisk in the butter. Pour the hot caramel over the chocolate and whisk to combine.

3. The sauce will keep in the refrigerator for up to 1 month. Reheat gently over low heat before serving.

MILK CHOCOLATE—COFFEE ICE CREAM

Our deliciously creamy Congo Coffee & Cream milk chocolate bar is the result of a partnership between Theo, Eastern Congo Initiative (ECI), and Congolese cocoa and coffee farmers. It's truly worthy of an ice cream in its honor. With 45 percent cocoa solids, our milk chocolate is luxuriously creamy, with deep, rich chocolate flavor. To make our Coffee & Cream bar, we add real ground Caffé Vita Congolese coffee. This heavenly ice cream is like a frozen dessert version of the bar—just as creamy, just as rich, with the same punch of deep chocolate and coffee flavor and the crunchy-chewy texture of real ground coffee.

MAKES ABOUT 1 QUART ICE CREAM—WE'RE A LITTLE TEMPTED TO CALL IT A SINGLE SERVING

¼ cup heavy cream

3½ ounces Theo 45 percent milk chocolate, chopped

2 cups half-and-half

½ cup sugar

5 large egg yolks

1 tablespoon finely ground Fair Trade coffee beans

1. To make a ganache, in a small saucepan over medium heat, bring the cream to a boil. Turn off the heat, add the chocolate, and let the mixture sit for 2 minutes. Use a whisk to blend the cream and the melted chocolate until perfectly smooth. Set aside.

2. To make the custard for the ice cream, in a medium saucepan over medium heat, combine the half-and-half and sugar, and bring to a boil. While it heats, whisk the egg yolks in a medium bowl until smooth. Keep a careful eye on the half-and-half mixture as it nears the boil, because it will froth up quickly. When the half-and-half mixture has reached a full boil, remove it from the heat and ladle about ½ cup into the bowl with the yolks, whisking constantly. Then pour the yolk mixture back into the saucepan with the half-and-half, whisking constantly until well blended. Cook the custard over medium-low heat, stirring gently and constantly with a wooden spoon or spatula, until the foam subsides and the custard thickens slightly and coats the back of the spoon. Strain the custard through a fine mesh strainer into a clean bowl to remove any bits of cooked egg. Add the ganache to the custard, using a clean whisk to combine.

3. Make an ice bath by putting a couple of cups of ice cubes in a large bowl with a few inches of cold water. Set the bowl of custard in the ice bath to cool, stirring occasionally. When it's cold, cover the custard and refrigerate for at least a few hours, preferably overnight.

4. Freeze the custard in an ice-cream maker according to the manufacturer's instructions. Just before removing it, sprinkle in the coffee and let the machine stir it in completely. You can serve the ice cream right away, or put it in an airtight container in the freezer to harden.

eastern congo initiative (ECI)

The Eastern Congo Initiative is a grant making and advocacy organization dedicated to creating social and economic development opportunities for the people of eastern Democratic Republic of Congo. Our partnership with ECI is born out of our shared belief that real, enduring change often comes from public-private partnerships. We're able to develop solutions that will improve lives in eastern Congo through our joint expertise: ECI has a history of working with the Congolese people to create economic opportunities that serve as a foundation for stability and success, and Theo has extensive experience building sustainable, Fair Trade supply chains around the globe. Together, to date, we have impacted thousands of cocoa farming families and their communities in positive ways, providing livelihoods and hope for the future. Today, more than half of Theo's cocoa supply comes from DRC, and there is Congolese cocoa in every product we make. Look for Theo Chocolate-ECI Vanilla Nib and Coffee and Cream chocolate bars. A portion of the purchase price from the sale of every bar benefits the hard working people of Congo.

MINT STRACCIATELLA ICE CREAM

This easy Philadelphia-style ice cream (made with just dairy, no eggs) calls for the same combination of mint found in our Mint 70 percent dark chocolate bar: spearmint and peppermint. Spearmint, recognizable by its large, bright, slightly fuzzy, lime-colored leaves, is the variety most commonly found in backyard gardens. Its flavor is fresh, grassy, and herbal. Peppermint, with its small, purplish leaves, is less abundant but has the refreshing, nostalgic flavor of a candy cane. If you can't find peppermint, you can make this with just spearmint.

Because it's made without eggs, this style of ice cream tastes light and very fresh, perfect to flavor with fresh mint and enjoy on a warm summer day. We finish it by drizzling in an entire melted Theo 70 percent dark chocolate bar at the end of churning. The chocolate freezes on contact with the ice cream and is broken into small pieces by the machine. This results in crispy little chocolate bits scattered throughout—a delightful texture the Italians call *stracciatella*.

MAKES ABOUT 1 QUART ICE CREAM

2 cups heavy cream, divided

1 cup whole milk

¾ cup sugar

½ cup finely chopped fresh spearmint leaves

2 tablespoons finely chopped fresh peppermint leaves (or 1½ teaspoons dried)

3 ounces Theo 70 percent dark chocolate, melted (see page 25)

1. In a medium saucepan, bring 1 cup of the cream, the milk, and sugar to a bare simmer, stirring to dissolve the sugar. Remove the pan from the heat, add both mint leaves, cover, and let the mint steep for 30 minutes.

2. Meanwhile, make an ice bath by putting a couple of cups of ice cubes in a large bowl with a few inches of cold water, and set aside.

3. After 30 minutes, pour the cream mixture through a fine-mesh strainer into a medium bowl. Press on the mint solids to release as much flavor as possible. Stir in the remaining 1 cup cream and set the bowl in the ice bath to cool, stirring occasionally. When the mixture is cold, cover it and refrigerate for at least 4 few hours and preferably overnight.

4. Transfer the mixture to an ice-cream maker and freeze according to the manufacturer's instructions. When the ice cream reaches soft-serve consistency, put the melted chocolate in a small resealable plastic bag and cut off a tiny bit of a corner (so that just a very thin stream of chocolate can escape). Drizzle the melted chocolate into the churning ice cream and let the machine stir it in and break it up. You can serve the ice cream right away, or put it in an airtight container in the freezer to harden. This style of ice cream melts quickly, so if you're serving it fresh from the machine, be sure to use chilled bowls.

BIG SPOON'S PROFITEROLES WITH BANANA—CARAMELIZED COCOA NIB ICE CREAM AND CHOCOLATE SAUCE

Chef Charlie Durham has cooked everything from upscale Italian and French bistro to gastropub fare, but when it came time for him to start his own venture, the cheerful Big Spoon food truck with its retro 1970s logo, he chose to specialize in comfort food. Now Charlie pretty much makes whatever it is you really feel like eating, when you most want to eat it: in the winter he serves steaming-hot soups and stews, and in the summer he dishes up a wide variety of homemade ice creams. The banana–cocoa nib ice cream in this recipe is one of our all-time favorites—and we've sampled a lot of ice cream.

Once you've mastered the profiteroles (which you can do pretty much just by making them once), you'll always have the makings of a yummy, easy, yet fancy dessert on hand. The ingredients are simple, and chances are you have them in your pantry and fridge right now. This is also a great make-ahead recipe. Profiteroles freeze well—simply reheat the empty puffs in a 350-degree-F oven until warm and crisp. Big Spoon's chocolate sauce also keeps well—pour any leftovers into an airtight container and refrigerate for up to three weeks. The sauce is dark and intense and can be served warm or at room temperature.

Note that you'll need to make the ice cream at least one day before you want to serve the profiteroles.

MAKES 10 SERVINGS (ABOUT 30 PUFFS, 1½ QUARTS ICE CREAM, AND 1½ CUPS SAUCE)

For the ice cream:

1⅔ cups heavy cream

1 cup milk

3 medium very ripe, very well mashed bananas (about 1¼ cups)

5 egg yolks

½ cup packed light brown sugar

1 teaspoon vanilla extract

½ cup caramelized Theo cocoa nibs (from Candied Nib and Soft Cheese Toasts, page 59), broken apart or chopped into smaller pieces

1. To make the ice cream, first make an ice bath by putting a couple of cups of ice cubes in a large bowl with a few inches of cold water, and set aside.

2. In a medium saucepan over medium heat, combine the cream, milk, and bananas, and bring to a simmer. Meanwhile, in a small bowl, whisk together the egg yolks and brown sugar until smooth and creamy. Add about 1 cup of the hot cream mixture to the yolk mixture and whisk well to blend, then pour it into the remaining hot cream mixture, whisking constantly.

3. Cook gently, over medium to medium-low heat, stirring constantly, until the mixture thickens into a custard thick enough to coat the back of a wooden spoon. The mashed bananas make it a little tricky to tell when it's thick enough, so use a candy thermometer to check the temperature—the cream should register about 170 degrees F.

4. When the custard is cooked, stir in the vanilla, then pour it into a clean bowl and chill it in the ice bath or in a shallow container, covered, in the refrigerator. Chill the custard until it's completely cold, preferably overnight, then transfer it to an ice-cream maker and freeze according to the manufacturer's instructions. When the ice cream is ready, stir in the cocoa nibs. Transfer the ice cream to an airtight container and freeze it until you're ready to serve the profiteroles.

5. To make the profiteroles, preheat the oven to 400 degrees F and line 2 baking sheets with parchment paper. Set aside.

6. In a medium saucepan over high heat, bring the water, butter, salt, and sugar to a boil. Add the flour and stir vigorously until the mixture forms a buttery ball, about 2 minutes. Transfer the dough to the bowl of a stand mixer fitted with the paddle attachment, and mix on low for 3 to 4 minutes to let it cool. Add 4 of the eggs, one at a time. The batter will break every time you add an egg, but just keep mixing until it gets smooth again before adding the next egg.

7. Use a piping bag fitted with a large plain tip, or 2 spoons, to place walnut-size pieces of dough 2 inches apart on the prepared baking sheets. In a small bowl, whisk the remaining egg with 1 tablespoon of water, and brush each puff with the egg wash. Bake each tray of puffs for about 20 minutes, rotating the pan halfway through the baking time, until they're golden brown and feel very light when you lift them. Allow the puffs to cool on the baking sheet, then store them tightly covered (or freeze them) until you're ready to use them.

8. To make the chocolate sauce, in a medium saucepan over medium heat, whisk together the cocoa powder, sugar, corn syrup, water, and salt until it comes to a boil. Remove the pot from the heat and stir in the chocolate until it's completely melted and the sauce is smooth. If you added ¼ cup water, use the sauce warm, or refrigerate it and reheat gently before serving. If you used ½ cup water, you can serve the sauce cold or at room temperature.

9. To assemble the profiteroles, use a serrated knife to cut the tops off each puff. Place 3 bottoms on each plate. Place a scoop of ice cream in each puff and balance the top of each puff on top of the ice cream. Pour a spoonful of chocolate sauce over each profiterole and serve immediately.

For the profiteroles:

1 cup cold water

7 tablespoons unsalted butter, cubed

1 teaspoon kosher salt

1 teaspoon sugar

1¼ cups (5⅔ ounces) all-purpose flour

5 large eggs, divided

For the sauce:

¾ cup (2¾ ounces) cocoa powder

½ cup plus 1 tablespoon sugar

½ cup light corn syrup

¼ cup water (or ½ cup if you'll be serving the sauce at room temperature rather than warm)

½ teaspoon kosher salt

2 ounces Theo 70 percent dark chocolate, chopped

drinking chocolate

♥ ♥ ♥

THIERRY RAUTUREAU'S CHOCOLAT CHAUD GRAND-MÈRE

This recipe for decadently thick, rich, creamy hot chocolate comes from Thierry Rautureau, "the Chef in the Hat," chef and owner of Luc and Loulay Kitchen and Bar in Seattle. When he was a boy growing up in France, this is (almost) the hot chocolate he'd enjoy for breakfast at his grandparents' farm. The original was made with freshly drawn milk from the cows next door, brought in by his grandfather, and served with homemade sliced bread toasted on a fork in front of the ashes in the fireplace, slathered with his grandmother's salted butter. It's what Thierry would like to have for his last meal.

Thierry calls this a contemporary version of his childhood favorite. While it's unlikely that your milk will be quite as fresh, he says that using our 70 percent dark chocolate adds an intense yet delicate flavor that's an improvement over the cocoa he remembers. At Loulay he serves it for breakfast with warm, freshly toasted brioche and plenty of butter. He encourages his guests to butter their brioche generously and dunk it in the hot chocolate. You can also serve the *chocolat* with extra hot milk on the side if you prefer it less thick and dunkable.

MAKES ONE EXTRAORDINARILY GENEROUS 1½-CUP SERVING

1. In a small saucepan, bring the milk and half-and-half to a boil. Whisk in the chocolate and sugar until the chocolate has melted and the mixture is perfectly smooth and covered with foam. Pour the hot chocolate into a serving cup or small teapot.

2. Toast the brioche slices and serve them warm with the butter on the side.

3. To eat, spread the butter generously on the brioche, dunk the brioche into the hot chocolate, and enjoy!

¾ cup whole milk

¼ cup half-and-half

2 ounces Theo 70 percent dark chocolate, very finely chopped or grated

2 tablespoons sugar (or more if you like it sweet)

♥ ♥ ♥

2 slices brioche

Salted butter, for spreading

CHOCOLATE HORCHATA

Horchata is a drink served ice cold all over Latin America and Spain. It's light and refreshing, and always milky in color although it doesn't always contain milk. Our version is closest to the traditional Mexican drink, although we've taken a few liberties, not the least of which is adding chocolate. The rice needs to steep overnight to extract its flavor, so be sure to start this the day before you want to serve it.

MAKES ABOUT 4 CUPS

1 cup uncooked long-grain white rice

4 cups (1 quart) water, divided

2 cinnamon sticks

¾ cup milk, divided

¼ cup packed light brown sugar

¼ cup granulated sugar

1½ ounces Theo 85 percent dark chocolate, chopped

1. Put the rice, 1 cup of the water, and the cinnamon sticks in a blender. Blend for about 1 minute, until the rice and cinnamon are coarsely chopped and the liquid looks very milky. Add another 1 cup water and blend for another minute. Add the remaining 2 cups water and refrigerate overnight.

2. If you make the chocolate addition right away, it can chill overnight and your *horchata* will be quick to assemble. You can wait until the next day, but remember that the chocolate will need to chill too.

3. To make the chocolate, in a small saucepan slowly warm ½ cup of the milk, the sugars, and chocolate over medium heat, whisking constantly. Bring the mixture to a gentle simmer and whisk for another 30 seconds. Whisk in the remaining ¼ cup milk, then chill completely.

4. The next day, mix the rice mixture and the chocolate mixture together in the blender in 3 batches, for 5 seconds each. Strain the *horchata* through a cheesecloth-lined sieve set over a medium bowl or wide-mouth pitcher and discard the solids. Serve over ice.

CASAMIGOS' THEO COCKTAIL

Longtime friends George Clooney, Rande Gerber, and Mike Meldman love tequila. On the rocks, by the shot, at times straight from the bottle. We're told tequila-filled nights with friends is how their tequila, Casamigos, was born. They worked on the creation of Casamigos with their master distiller in Jalisco, Mexico, hand-selecting 100 percent Blue Weber agaves, and aiming to make a tequila so smooth, its taste didn't have to be covered up with salt or lime. They've been drinking Casamigos with friends and family for over five years and never intended for it to go public. We're delighted to be invited to their party—after all, who can resist the blend of chocolate and tequila in a delicious cocktail?! A toast to our new amigos at Casamigos!

If you're in a hurry, want to practice a little modern gastronomy, or just want to use your whipped cream dispenser, the rapid infusion method is lightning fast and pretty cool. See the note at the end of the recipe on what equipment you'll need. However, we prefer the depth of flavor you get when you infuse the tequila at room temperature. After a day, the mouthfeel is silky-smooth and the aroma so intoxicating you might be tempted to put a dab behind your ears. If you can wait another day, the tequila will practically have become a cocktail all by itself!

MAKES 1 LUSCIOUS COUPE (AND ENOUGH INFUSED TEQUILA FOR ANOTHER 7)

1. If using the long infusion method, start infusing the tequila at least 24 hours before you want to serve it; the longer you can leave it, the more flavor it will take on. To make the infusion, put the tequila in a quart container with a lid. Add the chocolate, cinnamon, and vanilla bean, replace the lid, and shake well. Let the mixture sit at room temperature for at least a day (you can start tasting it after 12 hours). When the infusion has darkened in color; has a strong aroma of chocolate, cinnamon, and vanilla; and tastes as flavorful as you'd like it to, strain it through a fine mesh strainer into a small bowl. Discard the solids, line the strainer with a coffee filter, and strain again.

2. If using the rapid infusion method, put the tequila, chocolate, cinnamon, and vanilla bean in an iSi canister and screw on the top. Charge with the first charger and shake gently for 30 seconds. Remove the spent charger, insert the new one, and charge again. Gently shake again for 30 seconds, then let the canister rest for 90 seconds. Hold the canister upright and point it into a container to catch anything that comes out of it, then gently and slowly express

For the infusion:

16 ounces Casamigos Reposado tequila

3 ounces Theo 70 percent dark chocolate, finely chopped

3 cinnamon sticks, cracked into many pieces

½ vanilla bean, sliced lengthwise

♥ ♥ ♥

1 ounce heavy cream

2 ounces infused Casamigos Reposado tequila

1 ounce Bärenjäger honey liqueur

Cinnamon stick, for grating

(continued)

the air. When the canister is fully expressed, unscrew the top and strain the liquid through a fine mesh strainer. Discard the solids, line the strainer with a coffee filter, and strain again.

3. To make the cocktail, have ready a shaker filled with ice and a squeeze bottle for the cream. Put a coupe glass in the freezer.

4. Pour the cream into the squeeze bottle and keep it refrigerated while you make the cocktail. Pour the infusion and honey liqueur in the shaker and shake vigorously until chilled. Strain the mixture into the frozen coupe glass. Shake the heavy cream in the squeeze bottle until frothy (if it doesn't have a lid, be sure to keep your finger over the opening), then slowly and carefully squeeze a layer of cream to float on top of the cocktail. Grate a little cinnamon on top and serve immediately.

note: If you're using the rapid-infusion method, you'll need a ½ liter iSi whipped cream dispenser and 2 cream chargers.

HOT CAKES' SMOKED CHOCOLATE AND MEZCAL SHAKE

Autumn Martin, chef-owner of Hot Cakes Molten Chocolate Cakery in Seattle, was our very first chocolatier, and she says she learned everything she knows about chocolate during the nearly five years she spent in our kitchen. To this day we hold our relationship with her dear, and we're super impressed by everything she's accomplished. Autumn is, admittedly, obsessed with smoked chocolate. She started smoking it at Theo back in 2007, and she hasn't stopped.

At Hot Cakes, Autumn serves up a range of molten chocolate cakes, cookies, and boozy shakes like this one—many of which feature smoked chocolate. This shake is absolutely delicious—and the smoking technique can be applied to other chocolate recipes.

Note that the ice cream quantity is a range: if your ice cream is very airy, you'll need more to reach twelve ounces than if you're using a denser style. To make a nonalcoholic version of this shake, simply substitute milk for the mezcal.

MAKES ONE 12-OUNCE SHAKE

1. Before you assemble the shake, temper the ice cream by letting it sit on the counter until it's soft and a little squishy on the sides (this will make the creamiest milkshake). Put a tall glass in the freezer to chill.

2. In a small bowl, whisk the mezcal into the chocolate. When the chocolate is completely smooth, pour it into a milkshake cup or blender, add the ice cream and lime juice, and blend until just mixed—don't overmix, or you'll end up with a thin, bubbly shake. The less you blend, the thicker and creamier your shake will be. Pour the shake into the frozen glass and top with freshly whipped cream and a pinch of sea salt.

3 to 5 (3-ounce) scoops vanilla ice cream

1 ounce mezcal

2 ounces Theo 70 percent chocolate, smoked (instructions follow) and melted (see page 25)

½ teaspoon freshly squeezed lime juice

Whipped cream, for serving

Pinch sea salt, for serving

(continued)

how to smoke chocolate

To make a smoker, get 2 small cardboard boxes (about 8 by 8 by 8 inches) and 1 cardboard tube from a paper towel roll. Cut a tube-size circular hole in each box and insert an end of the tube into each hole, using packing tape to seal off any gaps. Line the inside of each box with aluminum foil, making sure the foil goes up the sides at least 3 inches.

Heat a couple of handfuls of wood chips in a sauté pan on the stove until they are evenly smoking. (Wood chips can be found at most grocery stores, alongside the charcoal; we like the subtle flavor of alder best, but you can use any kind you like.) Quickly place the smoking chips in one box, close the box, and seal it with packing tape. Fill the second box with a single layer of unwrapped chocolate bars, or you can spread a layer of chopped chocolate on a doubled-over piece of aluminum foil and place it in the bottom of the box. Close that box, seal it, and then smoke to taste. Autumn recommends at least 30 minutes, depending on how much chocolate you're smoking. Monitor the box with the chocolate inside to make sure the smoke is consistent and doesn't wane by peeking inside from time to time. You may need to replace the wood chips during smoking. To do so, simply remove the tape, scoop out the burned wood chips, fill with a fresh batch of smoking chips, close, and reseal the box.

ROASTED COCOA NIB—INFUSED VODKA

Chocolate martini, anyone? We love to keep a bottle of this in the freezer to serve plain as a digestif after dinner—or in a sugar-rimmed martini glass anytime. We recommend infusing the vodka for three days, but it starts taking on the color and aroma of the nibs almost immediately. Feel free to taste it every day, and if you're loving the results before the recommended three days have passed, by all means, strain it and enjoy.

MAKES 750 ML INFUSED VODKA

1 (750 ml) bottle of your favorite vodka

½ cup (2 ounces) Theo roasted cocoa nibs

1. Pour out about ⅓ cup of the vodka. Drink it, or put it aside in a closed container (you can add it back to the bottle later). Use a funnel to add the cocoa nibs to the bottle of vodka, screw on the top, and turn the bottle upside down a couple of times. Set aside to steep for about 3 days, turning it upside down a few times a day, or whenever you think of it.

2. After at least 3 days, strain the vodka through a mesh strainer lined with a triple layer of cheesecloth, discarding the cocoa nibs. Pour the nib-infused vodka through a funnel back into the bottle. Add the reserved vodka (if you still have it).

confections

♥ ♥ ♥

85 PERCENT NOIR GANACHE CONFECTION

This is a great recipe with which to begin your confectionary adventure. It will give you a chance to work with Theo chocolate and learn our ganache method. Prepare to be amazed by how silky-smooth this filling becomes when it sets.

MAKES ONE 8-BY-8-INCH PAN OF GANACHE (ABOUT 64 ONE-INCH SQUARES)

10 ounces Theo 85 percent dark chocolate, very finely chopped

4½ tablespoons cold unsalted butter, cut into ¼-inch dice

1 cup heavy cream

3 tablespoons honey

♥ ♥ ♥

About 2 pounds tempered Theo 70 percent dark chocolate (see page 28), for dipping

1. Line an 8-by-8-inch pan with parchment paper, leaving an overhang on all sides to facilitate unmolding the ganache once it has set. Put the chocolate in a heatproof bowl (such as stainless steel) set on a folded kitchen towel, to keep the bowl from slipping. Set the cold butter beside it.

2. In a small saucepan over medium-high heat, warm the cream and honey, stirring to dissolve the honey. Use a candy thermometer to carefully check the temperature of the cream. When it reaches 140 degrees F, remove the pan from the heat and pour the cream over the chocolate. Immediately start whisking the mixture vigorously and add about ½ tablespoon of the butter pieces. Continue adding the butter pieces every 5 to 10 seconds, and keep whisking vigorously, until all the butter has been added. If you can still see bits of butter, keep whisking. The whole process should take less than 2 minutes, and the finished ganache should be silky-smooth and have the consistency of pudding. (If the ganache breaks, see the tips on the opposite page.)

3. Quickly transfer the ganache to the prepared pan and use a small spatula (preferably a small metal offset spatula) to push the ganache into the corners. Tap the pan to smooth the top—only use the spatula if necessary, as too much agitation can break the ganache. Leave the pan for between 12 and 24 hours, uncovered, to set completely and crystallize before cutting the ganache and dipping it in the tempered chocolate (see Dipping Ganache Confections, page 34).

4. Once they're dipped, you can leave these confections as they are or decorate them with any number of flavorful accents; just be sure to apply the decoration before the tempered chocolate sets. We suggest candied flowers, toasted coconut, plain or candied cocoa nibs, nuts, candied coffee beans, smoked almonds, or a pinch of your favorite salt, just to get you started. The sky's the limit! The chocolate-coated confections will keep at room temperature for up to 2 weeks.

troubleshooting tips for ganache confections

When you're making a ganache, if you overhandle it, or if the liquid is too warm when you add it to the chocolate, it can break very easily (it will seem greasy instead of glossy and may even look curdled). Don't panic! Put the bowl in the freezer for 20 seconds, then take it out and whisk the ganache for 30 seconds. Repeat until the ganache becomes smooth again and starts to set.

If the liquid is too cool when you add it to the chocolate, or if you haven't chopped the chocolate finely enough, not all of it will melt. Just microwave the ganache for 10 seconds, then whisk it for 15 seconds. Repeat as necessary until the ganache becomes smooth.

FIG-FENNEL GANACHE CONFECTION

This combination of chocolate, red wine, dried figs, and fennel has won multiple gold medals due to its sophisticated deliciousness. It has the added bonus of superb texture—little crunchy fig seeds and chewy bits of fig.

Note that you'll make a bit more fig paste than is required for the recipe, so be sure to measure it before you add it. The leftover paste is a perfect accompaniment to a cheese plate, or use it like jam.

MAKES ONE 8-BY-8-INCH PAN OF GANACHE (ABOUT 64 ONE-INCH SQUARES)

For the fig paste:

¾ cup dry red wine (such as merlot)

½ cup sugar

4¼ ounces (about 13) dried Mission figs, stemmed and halved (or quartered, if large)

2¾ ounces (about 5) dried Calimyrna figs, stemmed and halved (or quartered, if large)

2 tablespoons freshly squeezed lemon juice

For the ganache:

1 tablespoon plus 1¼ teaspoons fennel seed

1 cup heavy cream

4½ ounces Theo 70 percent dark chocolate, very finely chopped

4 ounces Theo 45 percent milk chocolate, very finely chopped

♥ ♥ ♥

About 2 pounds tempered Theo 70 percent dark chocolate (see page 28), for dipping

1. First, make the fig paste. In a medium saucepan, bring the wine and sugar to a simmer. Add both types of figs and simmer gently, stirring occasionally, until they're tender and the syrup is thick like molasses, about 30 minutes. Remove the pan from the heat, add the lemon juice, and stir well.

2. Let the fig mixture cool slightly, then put it in the bowl of a food processor and puree it into a semi-smooth paste. The fig seeds should remain whole, but the fig pieces should be no larger than ⅛ inch. Measure out a generous ¾ cup (8.1 ounces) and set aside. Reserve the remaining fig paste for another use.

3. To make the ganache, roughly chop the fennel seed (you can use a spice grinder, but grind it very coarsely). In a small saucepan, bring the cream to a boil, then remove it from the heat. Stir in the fennel seed, cover the pan, and let the fennel steep for 45 minutes.

4. Meanwhile, line an 8-by-8-inch pan with parchment paper, leaving an overhang on all sides to facilitate unmolding the ganache once it has set. Put both chocolates in a heatproof bowl (such as stainless steel) set on a folded kitchen towel, to keep the bowl from slipping.

5. Strain the cream into a bowl, letting it drain by itself (don't press on the fennel solids). Discard the fennel, pour the cream back into the pan, and add the fig paste, mixing well. Reheat the cream mixture gently over medium-low heat. Use a candy thermometer to carefully check the temperature of the mixture. When it reaches 140 degrees F, remove the pan from the heat and pour the cream over the chocolate, stirring it together until thick and smooth.

6. Immediately transfer the ganache to the prepared pan and use a small spatula (preferably a small metal offset spatula) to press it into the corners—this ganache gets very stiff quickly, so work fast. Make sure the ganache evenly covers the bottom of the pan before smoothing the top. Leave the pan for between 12 and 24 hours, uncovered, to set completely and crystallize before cutting the ganache and dipping it in tempered chocolate (see Dipping Ganache Confections, page 34). The chocolate-coated confections will keep at room temperature for up to 2 weeks.

ganache confections

Visitors often ask us why our ganache confections are so velvely smooth, and why they melt in your mouth so beautifully. There are a couple of reasons. The first is that our chocolate contains absolutely nothing but cocoa solids, cocoa butter, organic vanilla bean, and sugar—except for our milk chocolate, which also contains milk powder. Unlike most chocolate manufacturers, we don't use soy lecithin as an emulsifier, so our chocolate melts on your tongue very evenly, with no waxy feel, and does so more quickly.

The second reason our confections are so luscious is that we table temper our fillings. We have found it to be the best way to maintain quality while making relatively large batches of ganache fillings by hand. We have also discovered that this process has other positive effects. Table tempering incorporates a little air, and the resulting product is lighter and smoother. Those tiny air bubbles also keep the ganache from shrinking as it crystallizes, so when we dip the confections in tempered chocolate and the chocolate sets, the coating doesn't crack.

The ganache table-tempering process goes like this: We gently warm the chocolate and butter in the recipe—not until it melts, but just until it softens. Then we heat the cream or fruit puree and pour it over the chocolate and butter. We stir this mixture until it's smooth and all the solids have melted (we call this mixture *ganache*), pour it out onto a marble-topped table, and use a large metal spatula to spread it as thinly as we can. We let it set for a bit, and then we scrape up the ganache and gather it together. As we repeat this process of spreading and gathering, the ganache breaks—it goes from looking smooth and glossy to looking oily and mottled, and it begins to turn from a liquid into a paste. Slowly, the ganache comes back together—the buttery slick gets reincorporated, and the ganache becomes smooth and thick. At this point, we spread the tempered ganache into a frame on a sheet pan and set aside to crystallize (set) overnight. If you have a marble or granite slab at home, you can try this with any of our ganache recipes. Tip: When you table temper, you don't have to worry quite so much about the temperature of the hot liquid called for in the recipe.

But we're going to assume that most people don't have a marble slab in their kitchen and/or don't want to spread ganache all over their counter, so we've adapted our recipes to be workable at home. In the process, we may or may not have had a few failures, so we've shared Troubleshooting Tips for Ganache Confections, page 187—we hope this will help you feel bolder about trying these recipes at home.

the confection kitchen

Every year we welcome more than 50,000 visitors. When you come on a tour, your visit first takes you through our factory, warmed by machines that clean, roast, winnow, grind, and conch cocoa beans to turn them into chocolate. Then your guide leads you through a set of double doors into a cooler version of heaven, our confection kitchen. It's where we play, experiment, and discover entirely new tastes and experiences, marrying our passion for chocolate with pure imagination.

While the change in temperature from one side of the factory to another might be the first thing you notice, the aromas that envelop you quickly steal your attention. Depending on the day, the prevailing bouquet might be fresh mint leaves steeping in cream, lemon peels being rasped by the dozen, coconut toasting in our oven, or buttery caramel roiling in a copper kettle.

You'll see Theo chocolatiers busy at work, surrounded by long stainless steel and marble-topped tables; induction burners and an oven; the copper kettle for our caramels, toffees, and brittles; and lots and lots of rack stands filled with sheet pans ready to hold the day's production of treats. The only machines you'll see, however, are a couple of mixers and an enrober (the machine that covers our confections with tempered chocolate)—visitors are frequently surprised to learn that we create all our confections by hand, using the chocolate being made just a few feet away on the other side of the factory wall.

The enrober features the closest thing we have to a chocolate waterfall—small in scale, but still gorgeous to look at. Its cooling tunnel has a conveyor belt inside that carries our hand-decorated confections to the packing room, straight out of the legendary *I Love Lucy* episode with chocolates flying everywhere. In reality, though, the confection packing room is one of the calmest and most orderly places in our entire factory.

BASIL GANACHE CONFECTION

We make this seasonal confection in the summertime, when fresh basil abounds. It may sound like an unusual flavor for a truffle, but basil's minty, licorice-y tones make it a perfect partner for chocolate. Our method for preparing ganache results in a particularly silky filling, but the addition of milk chocolate to this recipe makes it even silkier.

MAKES ONE 8-BY-8-INCH PAN OF GANACHE (ABOUT 64 ONE-INCH SQUARES)

1. In a small saucepan over medium-high heat, bring the cream and honey to a simmer, stirring to dissolve the honey. Remove the pan from the heat, stir in the basil, and cover the pan. Let the basil steep for 30 minutes.

2. Meanwhile, line an 8-by-8-inch pan with parchment paper, leaving an overhang on all sides to facilitate unmolding the ganache once it has set. Put both chocolates in a heatproof bowl (such as stainless steel) set on a folded kitchen towel, to keep the bowl from slipping. Set the cold butter beside it.

3. Strain the cream into a bowl, pressing on the chopped basil to squeeze out all the flavored cream. Discard the basil, pour the cream back into the pan, and reheat it gently over medium-low heat. Use a candy thermometer to carefully check the temperature of the cream. When it reaches 140 degrees F, remove the pan from the heat and pour the cream over the chocolate. Immediately start whisking the mixture vigorously and add about ½ tablespoon of the butter pieces. Keep adding the butter pieces every 5 to 10 seconds, and keep whisking vigorously, until all the butter has been added. If you can still see bits of butter, keep whisking. The whole process should take less than 2 minutes, and the finished ganache should be silky-smooth and have the consistency of pudding. (If the ganache breaks, see Troubleshooting Tips for Ganache Confections, page 187.)

4. Quickly transfer the ganache to the prepared pan and use a small spatula (preferably a small metal offset spatula) to push the ganache into the corners. Tap the pan to smooth the top—only use the spatula if necessary, as too much agitation can break the ganache. Leave the pan for between 12 and 24 hours, uncovered, to set completely and crystallize before cutting the ganache and dipping it in the tempered chocolate (see Dipping Ganache Confections, page 34). The chocolate-coated confections will keep at room temperature for up to 2 weeks.

¾ cup plus 2 tablespoons heavy cream

1½ tablespoons honey

1 ounce organic basil sprigs, leaves picked, washed, spun completely dry, and finely chopped

9¼ ounces Theo 45 percent milk chocolate, very finely chopped

3¾ ounces Theo 70 percent dark chocolate, very finely chopped

3 tablespoons cold unsalted butter, cut into ¼-inch dice

♥ ♥ ♥

About 2 pounds tempered Theo 70 percent dark chocolate (see page 28), for dipping

RASPBERRY GANACHE CONFECTION

Raspberry and chocolate is a match made in heaven. In the summer we bring in loads of fresh, ripe, local organic raspberries, which we puree, strain, and then portion and freeze so we can make batch after batch of these melt-in-your-mouth, sweet-tart treats. Out of season (like for Valentine's Day, hint, hint), we suggest you use frozen organic raspberries. Just let them thaw before you make and strain your puree.

MAKES ONE 8-BY-8-INCH PAN OF GANACHE (ABOUT 64 ONE-INCH SQUARES)

1. Line an 8-by-8-inch pan with parchment paper, leaving an overhang on all sides to facilitate unmolding the ganache once it has set. Put both chocolates in a heatproof bowl (such as stainless steel) set on a folded kitchen towel, to keep the bowl from slipping. Set the cold butter beside it.

2. In a small pan over medium heat, warm the raspberry puree and honey, stirring to dissolve the honey. Use a candy thermometer to carefully check the temperature of the puree. When it reaches 140 degrees F, remove the pan from the heat and pour the puree over the chocolate. Immediately start whisking the mixture vigorously and add about ½ tablespoon of the butter pieces. Keep adding the butter pieces every 5 to 10 seconds, and keep whisking vigorously, until all the butter has been added. If you can still see bits of butter, keep whisking. The whole process should take less than 2 minutes, and the finished ganache should be silky-smooth and have the consistency of pudding. (If the ganache breaks, see Troubleshooting Tips for Ganache Confections, page 187.)

3. Quickly transfer the ganache to the prepared pan and use a small spatula (preferably a small metal offset spatula) to push the ganache into the corners. Tap the pan to smooth the top—only use the spatula if necessary, as too much agitation can break the ganache. Leave the pan for between 12 and 24 hours, uncovered, to set completely and crystallize before cutting the ganache and dipping it in tempered chocolate (see Dipping Ganache Confections, page 34).

4. To decorate, in a small bowl, mix the freeze-dried raspberries and sugar together. After dipping 3 or 4 confections in tempered chocolate, sprinkle a pinch of the mixture onto each confection. Repeat with the remaining confections. The chocolate-coated confections will keep at room temperature for up to 2 weeks.

8 ounces Theo 45 percent milk chocolate, very finely chopped

6 ounces Theo 70 percent dark chocolate, very finely chopped

3½ tablespoons cold unsalted butter, cut into ¼-inch dice

¾ cup strained organic raspberry puree

1 tablespoon plus 1 teaspoon honey

♥ ♥ ♥

About 2 pounds tempered Theo 70 percent dark chocolate (see page 28), for dipping

1 ounce freeze-dried raspberries, finely ground for decoration

1½ teaspoons sugar, for decoration

BASIC TOFFEE

Caramelized sugar. Butter. Chocolate. Need we say more? Probably not, but we can't help ourselves. Crisp, crunchy, buttery toffee covered with chocolate is surely one of life's (simply) great pleasures.

Feel free to get creative with your inclusions, such as the ones we feature here: cocoa nibs, smoked almonds, and hazelnuts, all best sellers in our retail store. You can also sprinkle almost anything on the chocolate when you coat it: dried cherries, banana chips, or coconut are always well received and add chew. It's very hard to go wrong—just make sure there isn't too much moisture in the ingredients you decide to try.

We love Jacobsen Salt Co.'s sea salts (see Jacobsen Salt Co., page 137). Try sprinkling an interesting finishing salt on the chocolate coated side of your toffee before it sets, to create something really special.

MAKES ABOUT 1 POUND OF TOFFEE, BEFORE COATING

¾ cup (1½ sticks) unsalted butter, at room temperature

1 cup plus 2 tablespoons sugar

1 tablespoon plus 1 teaspoon light corn syrup

1 tablespoon water

♥ ♥ ♥

About 1 cup (for coating one side) or about 2 pounds (for dipping) tempered Theo milk or dark chocolate (see page 28)

1. Line a baking sheet with parchment paper or a Silpat mat and set aside.

2. Put the butter in a small (2- to 3-quart) saucepan. Sprinkle the sugar over the butter, and add the corn syrup and water. Cook the mixture over medium-low heat, stirring occasionally, until the butter has melted and the mixture is smooth. Continue cooking, without stirring, until it turns golden brown. If the toffee isn't cooking evenly and you need to stir it, do so gently, with a clean spatula.

3. Use a candy thermometer to carefully check the temperature of the toffee. When it reaches exactly 305 degrees F, immediately remove the pan from the heat and pour the toffee in an even layer onto the prepared baking sheet. When the toffee is cool, you can break it easily into uneven pieces, but if you prefer more regular pieces, score the toffee while it's still very hot by cutting into it with a large chef's knife. Don't be shy—if you barely mark the surface, your lines will disappear, so cut almost all the way through the hot toffee.

4. Set the toffee aside to cool completely and crystallize, for between 12 hours and 24 hours. As the toffee sits, a buttery sheen may develop on top of it, but eventually most of it will be reabsorbed. Before coating the toffee, turn it over and use a paper towel to wipe up any buttery sheen that remains, then coat in the tempered chocolate (see Dipping Toffees and Brittles, page 35). Stored in an airtight container or completely coated with chocolate, toffee will keep for up to 6 weeks. Toffee that is not completely coated and left uncovered will get sticky quickly.

variations

♥ ♥ ♥

COCOA NIB TOFFEE

½ cup (2 ounces) Theo roasted cocoa nibs, divided

¾ teaspoon *sel gris* (gray salt)

Follow the recipe for Basic Toffee. When the toffee reaches 305 degrees F, remove the pan from the heat and add one-third of the cocoa nibs and the salt, mixing well to incorporate. Pour the toffee in an even layer onto the prepared baking sheet. Immediately sprinkle on the remaining cocoa nibs (unless you're saving them to decorate the chocolate after coating), and use a clean spatula to gently press them into the toffee.

♥ ♥ ♥

SMOKED ALMOND TOFFEE

½ cup (3 ounces) smoked almonds, roughly chopped, divided

¾ teaspoon alder-smoked salt (such as Jacobsen Salt Co.'s)

Follow the recipe for Basic Toffee. When the toffee reaches 305 degrees F, remove the pan from the heat and add one-third of the almonds and the salt, mixing well to incorporate. Pour the toffee in an even layer onto the prepared baking sheet. Immediately sprinkle on the remaining almonds (unless you're saving them to decorate the chocolate after coating), and use a clean spatula to gently press them into the toffee.

♥ ♥ ♥

HAZELNUT TOFFEE

½ cup (2½ ounces) hazelnuts, toasted, skinned (if not DuChilly variety—
see note, page 61) and roughly chopped, divided

¾ teaspoon *sel gris* (gray salt)

Follow the recipe for Basic Toffee. When the toffee reaches 305 degrees F, remove the pan from the heat and add one-third of the hazelnuts and the salt, mixing well to incorporate. Pour the toffee in an even layer onto the prepared baking sheet. Immediately sprinkle on the remaining hazelnuts (unless you're saving them to decorate the chocolate after coating), and use a clean spatula to gently press them into the toffee.

CHRIS COSENTINO'S AGRODOLCE BRITTLE

Chris Cosentino, proprietor of Boccalone and Porcellino in San Francisco, is a swell guy as well as a James Beard Award–winning chef. Some years ago we did a very special project called Chef Sessions, a unique collection of confections formulated in our kitchen by seven of the West Coast's leading chefs, designed to benefit Food Lifeline. Chris joined us and brought a contagious enthusiasm that infected our kitchen with hilarity and fun. This recipe was his contribution, and to this day, it's one of our all-time favorite creations. Each of the flavors is so bright, but they harmonize beautifully. It's as special and unexpected as Chris himself.

MAKES 8 OUNCES OF BRITTLE, BEFORE COATING

⅔ cup sugar

2 tablespoons light corn syrup

1¼ tablespoons unsalted butter

1 tablespoon water

⅛ plus 1⁄16 teaspoon baking soda

2 tablespoons salt-packed capers, rinsed and air-dried overnight

2 tablespoons Zante currants

2 tablespoons pine nuts, lightly toasted in a dry skillet

♥ ♥ ♥

½ cup to ¾ cup tempered Theo 70 percent dark chocolate (page 28), for coating

Coarsely ground cocoa nibs, for decorating

1. Line a sheet pan with parchment paper or a Silpat mat and set aside.

2. In a small (about 1½-quart), heavy-bottomed saucepan over medium heat, combine the sugar, corn syrup, butter, and water. Use a silicone spatula to gently stir the mixture until it melts and becomes smooth. Try not to splash any of it onto the sides of the pan. Keep the spatula in hot water when not in use. Once the mixture is homogeneous and boiling, try not to stir it unless it appears to be cooking unevenly.

3. Use a candy thermometer to carefully check the temperature of the mixture. When it reaches exactly 305 degrees F, immediately remove the pan from the heat. Add the baking soda first, then the capers, currants, and pine nuts, and stir well. The mixture will foam up. Pour the brittle onto the prepared sheet pan, using the spatula to scrape the saucepan clean. Try to pour it in an even layer about ¼ inch thick (it will want to spread to this thickness anyway). Set aside to cool completely.

4. You can coat the brittle as soon as it's cool, but it's best if you can leave it for between 12 and 24 hours. It will eventually absorb the buttery sheen it makes as it cools. Coat the smooth side of the brittle in the tempered chocolate (see Dipping Toffees and Brittles, page 35). Before the chocolate sets, sprinkle it with the coarsely ground cocoa nibs. Because only one side of the toffee gets coated, and there is residual moisture in the capers, this toffee should be stored in an airtight container and enjoyed within 1 week.

tips for cooking sugar

For all the recipes in this chapter that involve cooking sugar, please be sure to have all your ingredients weighed out and ready to go, and all your utensils ready too, before you start the recipe. When you cook sugar, the temperature tends to rise quickly, plateau, and then rise quickly again. It's important to keep a constant, close watch, and be ready to move fast.

Whenever we cook sugar, we fill a small tub with very hot water and keep it next to our stovetop. Whenever we aren't stirring, we keep our utensil (spoon or spatula) in the water to dissolve the sugar clinging to it. That way, when you use the utensil, it will be clean. It's very important not to introduce sugar crystals to cooking sugar: you run the risk of crystallizing the entire pot of liquid sugar. This easy tip will ensure that never happens.

Another important thing to remember when cooking sugar is that it's extremely sticky. If melted sugar splatters or drips on you, it will cause a more serious burn than if you were splattered by a liquid that could be easily wiped off. Always use caution when cooking sugar: wear oven mitts whenever possible; stand back when you add liquids of any kind to hot sugar as the caramel will bubble and steam vigorously; and if you do get splattered, immediately hold the burn under cold running water—do not apply ice directly to a burn.

VANILLA CARAMELS

We make our caramel the traditional way, by hand, stirring it in a giant copper cauldron over a flame. It's labor intensive and something to see, but the results are well worth the effort. Rather than cooking all the sugar at once, we caramelize it bit by bit, developing flavor as we go. The result is a deep, dark caramel with a satisfying chew and the right balance between butter and sugar. There are few things better than the look on someone's face the first time they try one—it's always love at first bite.

MAKES ONE 9-BY-13-INCH PAN OF CARAMELS (ABOUT 96 ONE-INCH-SQUARE PIECES)

1. Cut the vanilla bean in half lengthwise. Use the back of a knife to scrape out the seeds from both halves. In a large saucepan, combine the seeds, bean, and the cream. Bring the cream to a simmer, then remove the pan from the heat, cover it, and let the vanilla steep for 20 minutes.

2. Meanwhile, line a 9-by-13-inch pan with a Silpat mat and lightly oil the sides of the pan. (Or you can line the pan with 2 strips of parchment paper, one lengthwise and one widthwise, both of them long enough to hang over the sides of the pan. Spray the parchment paper with nonstick cooking spray.)

3. Put the corn syrup in a bowl large enough to hold it as well as the cream. When the vanilla has steeped, return the pan back to the heat. Bring the cream back up to a simmer, then strain it over the corn syrup, pressing on the solids to extract as much of the flavor and seeds as possible. Cover the bowl with a piece of aluminum foil to keep the cream mixture warm, and set aside near the stove.

4. Put about ½ cup of the sugar into a large (at least 5- to 6-quart) heavy-bottomed pot, ideally a copper jam pot. Cook the sugar over medium heat without stirring until at least half of it has liquefied, then use a wooden spoon to gently stir it, incorporating the dry sugar into the melted sugar. When it has turned golden and there's no dry sugar left, sprinkle another ½ cup of the sugar over the surface of the caramelizing sugar and gently stir to incorporate. Repeat this, ½ cup sugar at a time, until you've incorporated all the sugar. Don't add more sugar until the previous addition has melted. If any lumps form, just press on them with the spoon and stir to let the bits melt.

½ vanilla bean

4¾ cups heavy cream

¾ cup light corn syrup

4½ cups sugar

½ cup (1 stick) unsalted butter, cut into 8 pieces

♥ ♥ ♥

About 3 pounds tempered Theo milk or dark chocolate (see page 28), for dipping (optional)

Flaked sea salt (such as Jacobsen Salt Co.'s), for decoration (optional)

(continued)

5. When all the sugar has been added, increase the heat slightly, and stir the caramel gently. It will go from looking opaque and grainy to shiny, smooth, more liquid, and the color will darken as well. When it's perfectly smooth, very liquid, and just beginning to smoke, add about 1 cup of the cream mixture. Be very careful—wear an oven mitt and stand back—the caramel will bubble and steam vigorously. Stir to thoroughly mix in the cream. When the steam has subsided and the bubbles are lavalike, velvety, and popping slowly, add another cup of the cream. Repeat this process until you've added all the cream. Be sure to wait at least 1 minute between additions to let the caramel heat up again. (If the caramel gets too cool, or the temperature fluctuates too much, it can crystallize or seize.)

6. Cook the caramel, stirring constantly and scraping the sides and bottom of the pot (a silicone spatula is good for this). Use a candy thermometer to carefully check the temperature of the caramel. When it reaches exactly 254 degrees F, turn off the heat, and quickly stir in the butter until fully incorporated. Carefully pour the hot caramel into the prepared pan. Set aside to cool completely, for at least 12 hours, before cutting.

7. To cut, turn the caramels out onto a chopping board. Spray a long, sharp knife with nonstick cooking spray and wipe off the excess (or just wipe the knife with a paper towel moistened with a little oil). Cut the caramels into long strips, wiping the knife between cuts and re-spraying it as necessary. Cut the strips across into squares. You can wrap the caramels in wax paper, or dip them in the tempered chocolate as you would dip ganache confections (see Dipping Ganache Confections, page 34), but without the thin chocolate precoat. Then, decorate them with a pinch of sea salt the way we do. The caramels will keep at room temperature for up to 3 months.

variation

♥ ♥ ♥

GHOST CHILI CARAMELS

Our Ghost Chili caramels are the proud recipients of a sofi Gold Award (the Oscar of the food world)! Infused with the flavor and slow-burning heat of ghost chilies—ranked among the hottest chili peppers in the world—they will blow your mind.

Dried ghost chilies are available at many specialty spice shops, usually sold by the ounce. We always wear gloves while handling them and strongly recommend that you do the same. The heat is in the chilies' oil, so be very careful when you discard the peppers after steeping them—they will still be extremely spicy.

To make Ghost Chili Caramels, follow the recipe for the Vanilla Caramels, substituting 2 dried ghost chilies (1.75 grams) for the vanilla bean and crushing the dried chilies into the hot cream. When straining the cream over the corn syrup, vigorously mash the chilies with a spoon or spatula to extract their flavor. Ladle some of the strained cream back into the strainer and mash the chilies again. Repeat a couple of times. Taste the cream—it should have a good kick. Continue with the rest of the recipe. The Ghost Chili Caramels should be dipped in tempered Theo 70 percent dark chocolate.

APPLE CIDER CARAMELS

We're constantly seeking a seasonal twist on our sweets, and this recipe is inspired by the mother lode of crisp, tart-sweet apples we enjoy every fall here in Washington State. Heavily reduced cider gives these chewy caramels plenty of apple flavor; the addition of just a little citric acid brings out the apples' tartness and cuts the sweetness of the caramelized sugar; and the spices add even more depth to a surprisingly complex-flavored morsel. A best seller in our shop every fall, they're such a delicious and different take on soft caramel that you may just find yourself making them all year round.

MAKES ONE 9-BY-13-INCH PAN OF CARAMELS (ABOUT 96 ONE-INCH-SQUARE PIECES)

1. Line a 9-by-13-inch pan with a Silpat mat and lightly oil the sides of the pan. (Or you can line the pan with 2 strips of parchment paper, one lengthwise and one widthwise, both of them long enough to hang over the sides of the pan. Spray the parchment with non-stick cooking spray.)

2. In a small saucepan over medium heat, simmer the cider to reduce it to ¾ cup. Check the volume periodically.

3. Put the corn syrup in a bowl that is large enough to hold it as well as the cream and cider reduction. Put the cream in a medium sauce-pan, add the cider reduction to it, and bring the mixture to a bare simmer. Pour the cream mixture over the corn syrup, cover the bowl with a piece of aluminum foil to keep the mixture warm, and set aside near the stove.

4. Put about ½ cup of the sugar into a large (at least 5- to 6-quart) heavy-bottomed pot, ideally a copper jam pot. Cook the sugar over medium heat without stirring until at least half of it has liquefied, then use a wooden spoon to gently stir it, incorporating the dry sugar into the melted sugar. When it has turned golden and there's no dry sugar left, sprinkle another ½ cup of the sugar over the surface of the caramel and gently stir to incorporate. Repeat this, ½ cup of sugar at a time, until you've incorporated all the sugar. Don't add more sugar until the previous batch has melted. If any lumps form, just press on them with the spoon and stir to let the bits melt.

5. When all the sugar has been added, increase the heat slightly, and stir the caramel gently. It will go from looking opaque and grainy to shiny, smooth, and more liquid, and the color will darken as well.

(continued)

4 cups apple cider

¾ cup light corn syrup

3¼ cups plus 3 tablespoons heavy cream

4½ cups sugar

½ cup (1 stick) unsalted butter, cut into 6 pieces

1 teaspoon ground cinnamon

½ teaspoon freshly grated nutmeg

½ teaspoon ground allspice

1 teaspoon citric acid

♥ ♥ ♥

3 pounds tempered Theo 70 percent dark chocolate (see page 28), for dipping (optional)

Spice mixture, for decorating (optional):

¼ cup sugar

1 teaspoon ground cinnamon

½ teaspoon freshly grated nutmeg

½ teaspoon ground allspice

When it's perfectly smooth, very liquid, and just beginning to smoke, add about 1 cup of the hot cream mixture. Be very careful—wear an oven mitt and stand back—the caramel will bubble and steam vigorously. Stir to thoroughly mix in the cream. When the steam has subsided and the bubbles are lavalike, velvety, and popping slowly, add another cup of the cream. Repeat this process until you've added all the cream. Be sure to wait at least 1 minute between additions to let the caramel heat up again. (If the caramel gets too cool, or the temperature fluctuates too much, it can crystallize or seize.)

6. Cook the caramel, stirring constantly and scraping the sides and bottom of the pot (a silicone spatula is good for this). Use a candy thermometer to carefully check the temperature of the caramel. When it reaches 258 to 260 degrees F, turn off the heat, and quickly stir in the butter. When the butter is incorporated, add the cinnamon, nutmeg, allspice, and citric acid, blending well. Carefully pour the hot caramel into the prepared pan. Set aside to cool completely before cutting, preferably overnight.

7. To cut, turn the caramels out onto a chopping board. Spray a long, sharp knife with nonstick cooking spray and wipe off the excess (or just wipe the knife with a paper towel moistened with a little oil). Cut the caramels into long strips, wiping the knife between cuts and re-spraying it as necessary. Cut the strips across into squares.

8. You can wrap the caramels in wax paper, or dip them in the tempered chocolate as you would dip ganache confections (see Dipping Ganache Confections, page 34), but without the thin chocolate precoat. After dipping, you can decorate the caramels with a pinch of the same spice mixture we use—just wait 30 seconds to 1 minute for the chocolate to start setting up. The caramels will keep at room temperature for up to 3 months.

theo chocolatiers

You'd think that working in a confection kitchen would cure chocolate cravings, but in fact, our confection team happily consumes chocolate daily! Testing new flavor combinations is an important part of our creative process, and taste is the ultimate master of flavor discovery. No idea is a bad idea in our kitchen—we have a highly collaborative approach to recipe development, and it's common for us to make many versions of a recipe before we get it right. Our ganaches and caramels have won gold medals all around the world, so we know we're reaching a standard of excellence that doesn't come easily.

MARSHMALLOWS

We love our marshmallows. They're light, fluffy, and sweet, and go down easy all year round. In summer, we pop them into the fridge or freezer for a cold, toothsome treat, and in winter we drop them into our drinking chocolate for an extra-special swirl. They're irresistible, and you don't have to be a kid to appreciate them. These are also the same marshmallows we use in our Big Daddy Marshmallow Bars (page 209), and it goes without saying they're the ultimate for making s'mores.

You can easily make these mint (we love them in our hot chocolate) by substituting mint extract for the vanilla this recipe calls for, or experiment with other flavors—any extract in your cupboard will work, as will rose flower water and orange blossom water.

MAKES ONE 9-BY-13-INCH PAN OF MARSHMALLOWS (ABOUT SIXTY THREE 1¼ INCH SQUARE PIECES)

1. Line the bottom of a 9-by-13-inch pan with a Silpat mat or parchment paper. Pour a nickel-size drop of vegetable oil in the center, and spread it all over the Silpat or parchment paper and up the sides of the baking pan. Set the pan aside. Connect the whisk attachment and bowl to a stand mixer.

2. Put the gelatin in a small microwave-safe bowl and add the cold water, stirring gently to combine. Set aside to soften.

3. Pour the corn syrup into a medium microwave-safe container, such as a 2- or 4-cup Pyrex liquid measuring cup, and heat in the microwave until the syrup is quite warm (almost hot) and very liquefied. Set aside next to the stove.

4. Put the sugar in a medium heavy-bottomed saucepan (at least 2 quarts, but no more than 4½ quarts, or it gets too difficult to measure the temperature of the sugar syrup). Add the water, stirring gently, without letting any sugar syrup splash onto the sides of the pan. Cook over medium heat, stirring occasionally to help the sugar melt evenly.

5. Meanwhile, melt the gelatin in the microwave until liquid. Don't overheat it. This will only take a few seconds—you may want to partially melt it, give it a stir, then melt it the rest of the way. Set aside next to the corn syrup.

Vegetable oil, for greasing

4 packets (1 ounce total) powdered gelatin

⅔ cup cold water

2 cups plus 1 tablespoon light corn syrup

2¼ cups sugar

⅔ cup water

½ teaspoon vanilla extract

¼ teaspoon kosher salt

Cornstarch, for dusting

(continued)

6. Use a candy thermometer to carefully check the temperature of the sugar syrup. When it reaches 238 to 240 degrees F, immediately turn off the heat and add the warm corn syrup, mixing gently, then stir in the gelatin.

7. Pour the hot sugar mixture into the bowl of the stand mixer and whisk it on low for about 10 seconds to mix the ingredients. Increase the speed to medium and whisk until the mixture is frothy and pale throughout, about 3 minutes. Increase the speed to high and whisk until the mixture turns white, about another minute. Add the vanilla and salt, whisk on low to blend, then increase the speed to high and whisk until the mixture is very thick and just warm, another 3 to 5 minutes. Pour the mixture into the prepared pan.

8. Allow the marshmallow to sit uncovered in a cool, dry place overnight to set and cure. (It will set up completely in 4 to 6 hours, but the flavor and texture will improve if you can muster the self-control to leave it overnight.)

9. When you're ready to cut the marshmallows, dust the top with cornstarch, then turn the pan upside down on a cutting board. Peel off the Silpat mat or parchment paper and dust the top again with cornstarch. Spray a long, sharp knife with cooking spray and wipe off the excess (or just wipe the knife with a paper towel moistened with a little oil) and cut 12 (1-inch) strips across the length of the block (each strip will be about 9 inches long). Wash and dry the knife as necessary between cuts. Turn the strips so that one of their sticky sides faces up, dust with cornstarch, then flip them all over and dust the other sticky side. Line up 4 or 5 strips and cut them into 8 cubes each, then repeat with the remaining strips. Sift some cornstarch into a bowl and toss a handful of marshmallows at a time to lightly coat the sticky sides, then shake them gently to remove the excess. Repeat with the remaining marshmallows. Stored in an airtight container at room temperature, the marshmallows will keep for 3 to 4 weeks.

BIG DADDY MARSHMALLOW BARS

Here's another Theo original, inspired by everyone's summertime, gather-round-the-campfire favorite: s'mores. To make these decadent, chewy, fluffy, totally over-the-top morsels, we start with a handmade graham cracker crust, add a layer of buttery, vanilla-infused caramel, and stack a marshmallow cloud on top—then we envelop it all in a blanket of dark chocolate. The recipe took many months to perfect, but Big Daddies have been a Theo favorite since the moment we introduced them—and now you can make them yourself! To make them gluten-free, see the note at the end of the recipe.

MAKES 18 CANDY BARS OR 54 "FUN-SIZE" CANDIES

1. To make the graham cracker crust, preheat the oven to 350 degrees F. Line an 8-by-8-inch baking pan with parchment paper or a Silpat mat and lightly oil the sides of the pan.

2. Put the flours, sugar, baking soda, and salt in the bowl of a food processor and pulse a few times to blend well. Add the butter and pulse until the mixture resembles cornmeal.

3. In a small bowl, stir together the honey and molasses. Add this mixture to the bowl of the food processor and process until completely mixed and no streaks of honey remain.

4. Press the dough into the prepared pan. It might not look like there is enough dough, but there is! Use a fork to prick the dough every inch or so. Bake until firm and deep golden brown, about 20 minutes. (Don't underbake: you want the crust to be crispy.) Set aside on a wire rack to cool completely.

5. To make the caramel, use the quantities listed here and follow the instructions for Vanilla Caramels (page 199) through step 5, then use a small (2- to 3-quart) saucepan to cook the caramel to make it easier to measure the temperature. After you've thoroughly mixed the butter into the hot caramel, pour the caramel over the crust (but don't scrape out the saucepan—the last bit of caramel will probably have cooked for too long in the residual heat of the pan, and it will get too hard when it sets). Allow the caramel to cool until it's just barely warm to the touch before you make the marshmallow.

6. To make the marshmallow, use the quantities listed on the following page and follow the instructions for Marshmallows (page 205),

(continued)

For the graham cracker crust:

7 tablespoons (2 ounces) all-purpose flour

3 tablespoons (1 ounce) graham flour

1½ tablespoons (¾ ounce) sugar

¼ teaspoon baking soda

⅛ teaspoon kosher salt

3 tablespoons cold unsalted butter, cut into ½-inch pieces

4 teaspoons honey

¾ teaspoon molasses

For the caramel layer:

¼ vanilla bean

1 cup plus 3 tablespoons heavy cream

3 tablespoons light corn syrup

1 cup plus 2 tablespoons sugar

2 tablespoons (¼ stick) unsalted butter, cut into ½-inch pieces

For the marshmallow layer:

1 packet (7 grams) powdered gelatin

3 tablespoons cold water

½ cup light corn syrup

½ cup plus 1 tablespoon sugar

3 tablespoons water

¼ teaspoon vanilla extract

Pinch kosher salt

Cornstarch, for dusting

♥ ♥ ♥

About 3 pounds tempered Theo milk or dark chocolate (see page 28), for coating

with these exceptions: use a small (2-quart) saucepan to cook the sugar to make it easier to measure the temperature. Cook the sugar over low heat until it has dissolved completely. When whisking the marshmallow, it will only take about a minute at medium speed to get the mixture frothy and pale. After adding the vanilla and salt, increase the speed to high and whisk until the marshmallow is thick and very white, about 3 minutes.

7. When the marshmallow is ready, move as quickly as you can to pour it in an even layer over the caramel (such a small amount will set up very quickly). Use a small metal offset spatula to push the marshmallow into the corners of the pan and get the top relatively smooth. As the marshmallow sits, it will level itself. Let the pan sit for between 12 and 24 hours, uncovered, to set.

8. Dust the top of the marshmallow layer with cornstarch and then follow the instructions in Dipping Candy Bars (page 35) to cut, coat, and dip the bars in the tempered chocolate. The bars will keep at room temperature for up to 3 months.

make gluten-free big daddy marshmallow bars!

¼ cup plus 2 tablespoons gluten-free flour (such as Bob's Red Mill)

3 tablespoons brown rice flour

2 tablespoons sugar

¼ teaspoon ground cinnamon

⅛ teaspoon xanthan gum

⅛ teaspoon baking soda

⅛ teaspoon kosher salt

1¾ tablespoons cold unsalted butter, cut into ½-inch pieces

¾ tablespoon molasses

2 teaspoons cold water

¼ teaspoon vanilla

- Preheat the oven to 325 degrees F.

- Begin by using the measurements listed here and follow the instructions in Theo Gluten-Free Graham Crackers (page 113) for mixing the dough. Press the dough into a prepared 8-by-8-inch baking pan lined with parchment paper or a Silpat mat with lightly oiled sides. It might not look like there is enough dough, but there is!

- Use a fork to prick the dough every inch or so. Bake until firm and deep golden brown, about 20 minutes. (Don't underbake: you want the crust to be crispy.) Set aside on a wire rack to cool completely.

- Proceed to step 5 of the recipe above to finish the marshmallow bars!

NOUGOTTAHAVIT

Because this recipe is basically a better, Theo-fied version of one of the most winning candy bars of all time (rhymes with *knickers*), we held a contest in the summer of 2014 to name it. The response was incredible—like our fans. It was difficult to choose a winner, but in the end we decided that "Nougottahavit" really said it all. It's practically impossible to resist this decadent candy bar: chewy caramel packed with peanuts and topped with dense European-style nougat. Consider it a success if you have any left before it's time to dip them.

Admittedly, this recipe has a number of moving parts, so you should try your hand at making caramel and marshmallow before you delve in here. This recipe is a lot less complicated than it looks, but a little experience with cooking sugar and moving quickly will go a long way. Be sure to read through the recipe and check that you have all the necessary equipment before you start—and note that you'll need two candy thermometers and a glass liquid measuring cup (such as a two-cup Pyrex) to complete the recipe.

MAKES SIXTEEN 1-BY-4-INCH BARS

1. Butter an 8-by-8-inch pan and line it with parchment paper, leaving an overhang to facilitate removing the finished candy. Butter the parchment paper and set the pan aside.

2. To make the caramel, spread the sugar in an even layer in a medium (3-quart) heavy-bottomed saucepan. Cook the sugar over medium heat without stirring until at least half of it has liquefied, then use a wooden spoon to gently stir it, incorporating the dry sugar into the melted sugar. Press on any big chunks with the spoon to crush them so they melt more quickly.

3. Meanwhile, either in a microwave or small saucepan over low heat, warm the cream and corn syrup together until fairly hot, and set aside near the stove.

4. When all the sugar has been added, increase the heat slightly, and stir the caramel gently. It will go from looking opaque and grainy to shiny, smooth, and more liquid, and the color will darken as well. When it's perfectly smooth and very liquid, add about one quarter of the hot cream mixture. Be very careful—wear an oven mitt and stand back—the caramel will bubble and steam vigorously. Stir to thoroughly mix in the cream. When the steam has subsided and the bubbles are lavalike, velvety, and popping slowly, add a little more of

(continued)

For the caramel layer:

1 cup sugar

1 cup heavy cream

¼ cup light corn syrup

1½ tablespoons unsalted butter

2 cups dry roasted peanut halves

Heaping ¼ teaspoon *sel gris* or other coarse salt

For the nougat layer:

3 tablespoons peanut butter

½ ounce cocoa butter, melted

1⅓ cups sugar

2 tablespoons light corn syrup

For the nougat whip:

1 egg white

2 teaspoons sugar

⅓ cup plus 1 teaspoon honey

2 tablespoons plus 2 teaspoons light corn syrup

the cream. Repeat this process until you've added all the cream. Be sure to wait at least 30 seconds between additions to let the caramel heat up again. (If the caramel gets too cool, or the temperature fluctuates too much, it can crystallize or seize.)

5. Cook the caramel, stirring constantly, scraping the sides and bottom of the pan (a silicone spatula is good for this). Use a candy thermometer to carefully check the temperature. When it reaches exactly 250 degrees F, turn off the heat and very quickly stir in the butter, peanuts, and salt until fully incorporated. Carefully pour the hot caramel into the prepared pan and use a silicone spatula to press it into the corners. Set the pan aside to cool for at least a couple of hours before making the nougat.

6. When the caramel layer is cool, make the nougat. Begin by warming the peanut butter in the microwave or in a small pan over low heat. Stir in the cocoa butter and set aside.

7. Next, combine the sugar, corn syrup, and enough water to fully moisten the sugar in a medium (3-quart) saucepan. Stir gently over medium heat until the sugar has melted. Increase the heat slightly and continue cooking the sugar, undisturbed, until it reaches about 200 degrees F.

8. While the sugar cooks, make the whip. In the bowl of a stand mixer fitted with the whisk attachment, whip the egg white with the sugar until firm peaks form. While the egg white is whipping, heat the honey and corn syrup in a very small saucepan over medium heat until it registers 255 to 260 degrees F on the candy thermometer. Note that this will happen quite quickly. If the egg whites are firm before the syrup is ready, reduce the speed of the mixer to low. With the mixer running, pour the honey mixture slowly into the whipped egg whites. Whip the mixture on high speed until it's white and very fluffy, about 3 minutes. If necessary, you can reduce the mixer speed to medium while you wait for the sugar to cook.

9. At this point, the sugar syrup should be nearly ready—use a candy thermometer to carefully check the temperature. When it reaches 305 to 310 degrees F, pour the syrup into a 2-cup glass liquid measuring cup (to stop the cooking and also to facilitate adding it to the whip).

10. Add the hot sugar syrup to the whip in a constant stream with the mixer running, without letting the syrup hit the moving whisk. (An easier method is to add the syrup in 4 or 5 additions, turning off the mixer for each addition, but turning it back up to high immediately after and whipping for about 5 seconds between additions.) When all the syrup has been added, continue to whip for about 1 more minute, until the syrup is fully incorporated. Switch to the paddle attachment and beat in the warm peanut butter–cocoa butter mixture on low speed, just until combined, about 1 minute. The nougat (you just made nougat!) will still be quite warm.

11. Immediately pour the nougat on top of the caramel as evenly as you can, using a buttered spatula to spread it evenly. This layer doesn't have to be perfect, as the nougat will settle a bit before it cools.

12. Let the nougat set for at least 12 hours (but for no more than 24 hours). Then cut the nougat into 1-by-4-inch bars and dip them in the tempered chocolate (see Dipping Candy Bars, page 95). If you want your Nougottahavits to be just like ours, flip them over and dip them with the caramel layer on top. The chocolate-coated candy bars will keep for up to 3 months.

PEANUT BUTTER BUDDIES

We're downright determined to make a better version of all the candy bars we loved as kids, using quality ingredients. This is a seriously dangerous recipe—you can have a whole pan of flaky, peanut buttery, sweet-and-salty candy cooling on your countertop in less than fifteen minutes. It would take you longer to run down to the corner store to pick up the manufactured version, and it doesn't begin to compare. You've been warned.

We use CB's Nuts (see page 122) organic peanut butter to make these candies in our kitchen; we love the little bits of peanut in their "creamunchy" grind. We also use Himalayan pink salt, but you can use any relatively large crystal salt, including *sel gris* (gray salt) or flaked sea salt.

MAKES ONE 8-BY-8-INCH PAN OF CANDY (ABOUT THIRTY-SIX 1¼-INCH PIECES)

1½ cups peanut butter

¾ teaspoon pink salt

1⅓ cups sugar

⅓ cup plus 1½ tablespoons light corn syrup

½ cup water

♥ ♥ ♥

About 2 pounds tempered Theo milk or dark chocolate (see page 28), for dipping

1. Line the bottom of an 8-by-8-inch pan with parchment paper, leaving an overhang on one side to facilitate lifting it out of the pan. Put the peanut butter and salt in a small microwave-safe container and microwave until it feels very warm to the touch, stirring once or twice. Cover to keep warm and set aside next to the stove.

2. Put the sugar, corn syrup, and water in a medium-size heavy-bottomed pot. It should hold at least 2½ quarts, but measure no more than 9 inches across (or the sugar syrup will be too shallow to get an accurate temperature reading). Cook the mixture over medium heat, stirring occasionally. When the bubbles start to slow and thicken, start watching the temperature.

3. Use a candy thermometer to carefully check the temperature of the mixture. When it reaches exactly 305 degrees F (it will have just barely begun to take on a pale-yellow hue), immediately turn off the heat and add the very warm peanut butter mixture. Use a silicone spatula to gently but quickly fold (not stir) in the peanut butter. Work as quickly as you can (the folding process should take about 1 minute), but be sure to incorporate all the streaks of sugar syrup.

4. Quickly pour the hot candy into the prepared pan and use a silicone spatula to press the candy into the corners and flatten it. As soon as it's relatively smooth, use a heavy knife to score or cut into the still-soft candy to mark however many pieces you'll want (cut almost all the way through). Set aside to cool and crystallize for at

least 12 hours (but for no more than 24 hours). The candy will become flakier as it sits. Once it has cooled, cover it loosely with plastic wrap until you are ready to dip it.

5. When you're ready to dip it, lift the candy out of the pan and break it along the score lines. Dip the pieces in the tempered chocolate as you would dip ganache confections (see Dipping Ganache Confections, page 34), but without the thin chocolate pre-coat. The chocolate coated candy will keep at room temperature for up to 3 months.

index

♥ ♥ ♥

Hot Fudge Sauce, Chocolate-Stout-
  Caramel, 162, *163*

conversions

♥ ♥ ♥

VOLUME			LENGTH		WEIGHT	
UNITED STATES	METRIC	IMPERIAL	UNITED STATES	METRIC	AVOIRDUPOIS	METRIC
¼ tsp.	1.25 ml		⅛ in.	3 mm	¼ oz.	7 g
½ tsp.	2.5 ml		¼ in.	6 mm	½ oz.	15 g
1 tsp.	5 ml		½ in.	1.25 cm	1 oz.	30 g
½ Tbsp.	7.5 ml		1 in.	2.5 cm	2 oz.	60 g
1 Tbsp.	15 ml		1 ft.	30 cm	3 oz.	90 g
⅛ c.	30 ml	1 fl. oz.			4 oz.	115 g
¼ c.	60 ml	2 fl. oz.			5 oz.	150 g
⅓ c.	80 ml	2.5 fl. oz.			6 oz.	175 g
½ c.	125 ml	4 fl. oz.			7 oz.	200 g
1 c.	250 ml	8 fl. oz.			8 oz. (½ lb.)	225 g
2 c. (1 pt.)	500 ml	16 fl. oz.			9 oz.	250 g
1 qt.	1 l	32 fl. oz.			10 oz.	300 g

TEMPERATURE				11 oz.	325 g
OVEN MARK	FAHRENHEIT	CELSIUS	GAS	12 oz.	350 g
Very cool	250–275	130–140	½–1	13 oz.	375 g
Cool	300	150	2	14 oz.	400 g
Warm	325	165	3	15 oz.	425 g
Moderate	350	175	4	16 oz. (1 lb.)	450 g
Moderately hot	375	190	5	1½ lb.	750 g
	400	200	6	2 lb.	900 g
Hot	425	220	7	2¼ lb.	1 kg
	450	230	8	3 lb.	1.4 kg
Very Hot	475	245	9	4 lb.	1.8 kg

about the authors

JOE WHINNEY
Founder and CEO of Theo Chocolate

As a conservation volunteer in Central America working alongside Mayan cocoa farmers, Joe realized that social, economic, and environmental degradation are business-related problems. Joe's commitment to creating change in the world was galvanized after his first trip to West Africa in the midnineties where he witnessed poverty and economic oppression on a massive scale. In 1994, Joe began to pioneer the organic chocolate industry in North America through his love of chocolate and his passion for social and environmental justice. Joe expanded his work in 2005 by founding Theo Chocolate, the first Fair Trade and organic bean-to-bar chocolate maker in the Americas, which produces a wide variety of award-winning chocolate and confections.

DEBRA MUSIC
Co-Founder and CMO of Theo Chocolate

Debra's background includes extensive work as a social marketing and brand consultant. Since 2005, she has leveraged her business experience and creative sensibilities to launch and grow Theo Chocolate. Theo was born out of the desire to show chocolate lovers how organic, Fair Trade chocolate can positively impact the world, from the farmers who cultivate the beans to the consumers who support this beloved national brand. Debra's belief that we are all connected is at the very heart of Theo's business.

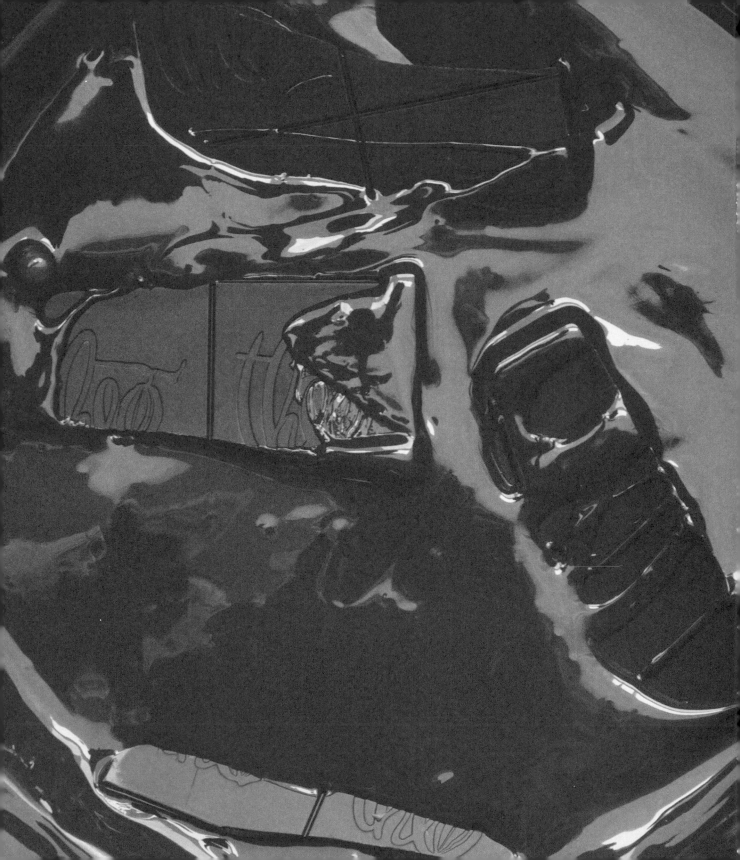